C000171735

Chinese Alchemy

Chinese Alchemy

Jean Cooper

Taoism, the Power of Gold,
and the Quest for Immortality

WEISER BOOKS

This edition first published in 2016 by Weiser Books
an imprint of Red Wheel/Weiser, LLC
With offices at:
65 Parker Street, Suite 7
Newburyport, MA 01950
www.redwheelweiser.com

Copyright © 2016 by J. C. Cooper

All rights reserved. No part of this publication may be reproduced or transmitted in any form or by any means, electronic or mechanical, including
photocopying, recording, or by any information storage and retrieval system,
without permission in writing from Red Wheel/Weiser, LLC. Reviewers may
quote brief passages. Originally published in 1984 by Aquarian Press, a part
of the Thorsons Publishing Group, ISBN: 1-85030-327-3.

ISBN: 978-1-57863-577-1

Library of Congress Cataloging-in-Publication Data

Names: Cooper, J. C. (Jean C.) author.
Title: Chinese alchemy : Taoism, the power of gold, and the quest for
  immortality / J.C. Cooper.
Description: San Francisco : Weiser Books, 2016. | Includes bibliographical
  references and index.
Identifiers: LCCN 2015042587 | ISBN 9781578635771 (5 x 7.75 pbk. : alk.
paper)
Subjects: LCSH: Taoism--China. | Alchemy.
Classification: LCC BL1923 .C66 2016 | DDC 299.5/14--dc23
LC record available at http://lccn.loc.gov/2015042587

Cover design by Graham Lester
Text design by Jane Hagaman

Printed in the United States of America
M&G

10 9 8 7 6 5 4 3 2 1

CONTENTS

ACKNOWLEDGMENTS

I am greatly indebted to Professor Needham for permission to quote, and use illustrations, from his monumental work *Science and Civilization in China*. My thanks also to Mr. W. Greenhalgh for reproducing photographs from old slides taken in China.

In memoriam

Francis Clive-Ross

ORIGINS

There is little in Chinese alchemy that cannot be associated with Taoism and although the exact origins of that alchemy may still be in dispute in the light of present incomplete evidence, it is not questioned that it grew and was nourished in the soil of popular and religious Taoism. It is also recognized that there are two distinct branches of Taoism: the classical *Tao Chia*, the mystical, metaphysical aspect, stemming from Lao Tzu and Chuang Tzu, and the popular, religious, magical, alchemical side, the *Tao Chiao*, which arose traditionally with the Yellow Emperor and his Three Immortal Ladies, or Maids, who taught him magic, mysticism and love. Lao Tzu and Chuang Tzu probably represented a movement against these earlier animistic-magico practices and founded the *Tao Chia* as a protest, or rather a correction, at a time when such practices had lost their original meaning and become loaded with superstition.

Yet another viewpoint is that classical Taoism was original but was too austere and rarefied for the general populace and later, meeting the shamanism which flourished in the tribes of the regions north and west of China proper, absorbed shamanistic-animistic lore and degenerated into the religious, ritualistic, magical and alchemical branch, the *Tao Chiao*, which fulfilled the day-to-day needs of the people and which still exists in modern times as a popular religion. Thus, from being abstract philosophy, it became a concrete religion with a ceremonial Church, having a priesthood, liturgy and theology, a Pope, and a Trinity known as the Three Pure Ones. From the original non-theistic mysticism it became not only theistic but polytheistic, adopting the pantheon of popular Buddhism.

While the origins and dates of Chinese alchemy are still being researched and debated (there are literally hundreds of Taoists texts as yet untranslated) it is known for certain that it flourished well before 144 BC, for at that date the Emperor issued an edict which ordered public execution for anyone found making counterfeit gold. The making of counterfeit cash was also proscribed. However, in the year 60 BC the then Emperor appointed a well-known scholar, Liu Hsiang, as Master of the Recipes so that he could make alchemical gold and prolong the Emperor's life. He failed to make the gold and so was disgraced. This points to an already well-established and widespread practice in alchemy. It was also said to have been practised in the fourth century BC by Tsou Yen, who had a reputation as a miracle-worker and a following among the aristocracy. He was also reputed to have been the first alchemist to combine the search for the Elixir with the search for gold.

The Later Han dynasty (AD 25-220) was a time of great interest in science, astronomy, botany, zoology and medicine and in this period there appeared the first book on alchemy, the *Ts'an T'ung Ch'i* of Wei Po-yang. Its date was about AD 142 and its title is translated as 'The Book of the Kinship of the Three,' but it was written in terms which were too difficult for the understanding of all but initiates. But most of the alchemical texts derive from the T'ang dynasty (AD 618-960), which maintained this interest, especially in the alchemical branch of Taoism.

The language of the *Ts'an T'ung Ch'i* being too complicated and esoteric to be of general use, it is to Ko Hung that we must turn for the earliest complete treatise. He lived about AD 260 to 340 and is regarded as the most famous of writers on Chinese alchemy. He is supposed to have written several hundred books but his known work is the *Pao P'u Tzu nei p'ien,* usually referred to as the *Pao P'u Tzu,* though this was, in fact, a pseudonym he adopted and can be translated as 'The Master who preserves his pristine simplicity,' which has also been rendered as 'Old Sobersides.' The work is in two parts, the *nei p'ien,* comprising some twenty scrolls, and the *wei p'ien,* some fifty. He says: 'My *nei p'ien,* telling of gods, genii, prescriptions and medicines, ghosts and marvels, transformations, maintenance of life, extension of years, exorcising evils and banishing misfortune, belongs to the Taoist school. My *wei p'ien,* giving an account of success and failure in human affairs and of good and evil in public affairs, belongs to the Confucian school.'[1]

It was Ko Hung who was responsible for the delightful definitions of classical Taoism and Confucianism. He was asked: 'Of Confucianism and Taoism, which is the more difficult?' He replied: 'Confucianism is difficulty in the midst of facility; Taoism is facility in the midst of difficulties; in it all annoyances are lifted with an inner harmony that grows of itself; perfect freedom of action and thought; no fear, no grief.' Taoists 'reject specialization in worldly matters, wash away all trickeries, forget wealth and neglect honours, block repression and encourage free expression, are not concerned about the loss of anything, do not glory in success and are not saddened by denigration and take no delight in praise.'

Ko Hung regarded the existing scrolls for medicines as incomplete, confused and often lacking in treatment for many critical illnesses. He said that they employed expensive ingredients only available to the rich, whereas his scrolls would be found to mention all the medicines and give full treatment for all serious illnesses: 'Any household possessing this book can dispense with the services of a physician. Further, it is not always possible to find a physician at a moment's notice and when you do find one he may not wish to come immediately.' (This strangely modern passage was written nearly 2000 years ago!)

Chinese alchemy, being more concerned with longevity and immortality than with the making of gold, was naturally involved with finding the Elixir of Immortality and with prescriptions for prolonging life. When challenged that he was attempting the impossible in trying to overcome mortality in this life, Ko Hung replied that although the deaf could not hear thunder or appreciate music, and the sun and the splendour of the Emperor's robes were invisible to the blind, it did not mean that these things did not exist. His recipe for long life was the use of appropriate medicines, breathing exercises and philosophical thought. Alchemy, like all esoteric lore, had to be learned from an adept and Ko Hung's master, Cheng Yin, at over eighty, had black hair, a 'full cheerful face' and could draw a strong cross-bow and shoot a hundred paces; he walked hundreds of miles and could drink two demijohns of wine without becoming drunk; he climbed mountains with agility and crossed precipitous places and dangerous heights which daunted younger men. He ate and drank the same things as anyone else, but could go for unlimited days without food and without feeling hunger.

In his writings Ko Hung maintained that alchemical change was only one facet of the universal transformations in Nature. 'It is clear, therefore, that transformation is something spontaneous in Nature. Why then should we demur at the possibility of making gold and silver from other things? Look at the fire obtained from heaven with the burning-mirror, and the water got at night [dew] from the moon-mirror; are they different from ordinary fire and water? . . . I guarantee that mercury can vapourize and that gold and silver can be sought successfully . . . the Manuals of the Immortals tell us . . . that it is in the nature of gold and silver that one can make them.' In his time there were treatises which contained recipes and formulae for 'melting jade,' 'transforming gold' and making 'talisman water.' But these obscure and probably esoteric terms notwithstanding, Professor Needham, the great authority on the development of Chinese science, says that Ko Hung's *Pao P'u Tzu* 'contains some scientific thinking at what appears to be a high level.'

Ko Hung disapproved of the recluse-alchemists seeking their own immortality to the neglect of their dependents, as so many did: 'To turn one's back upon wife and children and make one's abode in the mountains and marshes, uncaringly to reject basic human usage . . . is hardly to be encouraged. If by some good fortune they can become immortal and still go on living at home, why should they seek to mount specially to the heavens?' Once the preparation of the divine Elixir has been achieved successfully 'you and your whole household, not just you alone, will become immortals.' He also says that this state of immortality cannot be attained without good deeds, loyalty, friendliness and trustworthiness.

This condition of immorality was known as that of the *hsien,* the genie or immortal, and the alchemist aimed at achieving *hsien*-hood, of which there were several grades, as will be seen later. Strangely, Ko Hung's death was said to be consistent with the lowest grade, the *shih chieh hsien,* the 'corpse free,' one whose corpse disappears, leaving only the clothes or some identifying object behind. At his death he was encoffined but later it was found that his body had disappeared, only his clothes remaining.

While Ko Hung, Wei Po-yang and other early alchemists can be traced in historical records, many of the early names and the stages of alchemy are found only in legend, for which the Chinese have the delightful phrase 'wild history.' The most important of these legendary characters is undoubtedly the Yellow Emperor, Huang Ti, who traditionally reigned from about 2704 to 2595 BC. He was regarded as the first and greatest of Taoist immortals and alchemists and was said to have learned, not only from his Three Immortal Maids, but also from

Chang Tao-ling founder of the popular Taoism and the first Taoist pope

an Immortal who lived on a mountain, who, after considerable persuasion, instructed the Emperor in the understanding of the Tao, of sciences, meditation and medicines. Huang Ti was reputed to have written the Inner Classics. He became an Immortal, or *hsien,* himself and after reigning for over a hundred years he ascended to heaven on the back of a dragon, taking with him some seventy members of his domestic household and court, in full view of the populace. Others of his retainers, anxious to go heavenward with him, hung on to the whiskers of the dragon, but they gave way and the hangers-on, together with the Emperor's bow, fell to the ground. The people gazed at the Emperor and dragon until they disappeared into the heavens. The fallen bow was collected and venerated. Although there was a tomb and a shrine built for the Yellow Emperor it was said that it was later found to be devoid of a corpse and contained only a sword and shoes.

Another legendary character was the Emperor Yü the Great, traditionally known as 'the happy miner.' He was a smelter who 'pierced the mountains' and 'made the earth healthy.' He knew the difference between male and female metals and employed the *yin-yang* principles in all his work, dividing his cauldrons into *yin* and *yang*. There were nine of these, four *yin* and five *yang*. Here it is of interest to note the early appearance of the *yin-yang* doctrine, the importance of the number nine, which runs through all alchemy and Chinese lore, and the division of the number into even (*yin*) and odd (*yang*) numbers. As we shall see, the *yin-yang* symbolism is employed right through Chinese alchemy as the two powers of mercury and sulphur, the lunar and solar.

The legendary accounts of the origins of alchemy are not confined to the Chinese 'wild history;' in the West there is the story that fallen angels were responsible for teaching the science of alchemy to the women they married on earth. Another tradition claims that alchemy owed its inception to Hermes, the Egyptian Thoth, God of Wisdom, or that Isis won the secret from an angel in return for sexual favours, and handed it to her son Horus. Yet another legend is that God revealed the secrets of alchemy to Moses and Aaron, both master magicians.

ALCHEMY EAST AND WEST

Chinese alchemy, while often running parallel with that of the West, and showing considerable similarity with Indian beliefs, for example the idea of a drug which could prolong life, the Elixir of Immortality, which appears in India a thousand years before Christ, holds no definite proof of common origins, but much of exchange of thought. The same argument rages over the beginnings of alchemy as over symbolism: whether such ideas and symbols 'migrated' from one country to another in trading and cultural contacts, or arose spontaneously in different civilizations and widely separated parts of the world.

In view of the universal similarities in the content and types of dreams and in the workings of the subconscious mind, as demonstrated by Jung's work, it is reasonable to suppose that in waking life the same types and ideas also rise spontaneously in the human mind. In mythology, religion, symbolism, fairy tale and folklore and such early sciences as alchemy and astrology, while the local colouring of dreams and thoughts is naturally different, the basic contents, symbolism and psychological implications appear to be universal; but while there are similarities, there are also differences in East and West. The answer to the question of migration versus spontaneous growth lies probably in a degree of both. Military conquests, trade and cultural exchanges obviously spread ideas and knowledge, while, on the other hand, it is only natural that people the world over should have asked the same questions about their environment, the cosmos in which they lived and their relationship with it.

There seems to have been a considerable exchange of knowledge between China and India; it is known that alchemical practices were prevalent in both countries well before the Christian era and there was definite evidence of exchange when a Chinese Emperor of the T'ang dynasty sent an envoy, Wang Hsüan-tse, to India between AD 643 and 665; there are indications that he made two visits during this time. He was a specialist in prolonging life—that is to say, an alchemist—and a noted magician. He brought back with him an Indian Brahmin, Narayamasvamin, who was an alchemist and physician, while another Indian magician came over from Kashmir in 664-5 on the orders of the Emperor Kao Tsung: this magician was thought to have possessed the drug of longevity. Waley maintains that there is no doubt that 'a definite give and take went on between China and India during the T'ang dynasty,' but that Chinese techniques were already well developed long before any known contact with India.

Other branches of early alchemy were established in Babylonia and Chaldea; the Persians were skilled in magic, alchemy and medicine, while from Egypt came the great Hermetic tradition which passed to Greece, Greek culture being spread widely later by the conquests of Alexander the Great. Arabian alchemy also rose from the Alexandrian School in Egypt but was, at the same time, in touch with Chinese thought. From Greek and Arabic culture alchemy spread into Europe, but showed a direct inheritance from Hermes/Thoth. Arabic and Byzantine alchemy were, like the ancient Hellenic practices, a mixture of magic, astrology and mysticism touched with the tradition of Hermes Trismegistus.

Some authorities have maintained that all alchemy came from China originally and spread westward later; others believe that it arose in Egypt. Babylon has also been suggested as the source, while others again, as has been said, have propounded the theory that the same ideas and concepts arose spontaneously and existed simultaneously in different countries. However, the idea most basic to Chinese alchemy, the Elixir of Life, did not appear in the West until the twelfth century AD, when it was introduced there from China by the Arabs.

Similarities between eastern and western alchemy are seen in the concept of polarity and the universal symbolic reverence for gold as the great solar power, with its counterpart in the lunar silver. The Sol and Luna theme, presented in various guises, runs through all alchemy: Fludd, for instance, expressed this polarity as the Sun, the father, the heart, the right eye, with the left eye as the Moon, the mother, the womb, as well as the basic duality of sulphur and quicksilver. All branches of alchemy reverenced the Earth, the Great Mother, in whose womb were nourished the metals and from which they were born.

The essential difference between Chinese alchemy and that of the West was that while the latter was always associated with gold, whether in the transmutation of base metals into gold or the transformation of the base metal of unregenerate man into the pure gold of the spiritual life and realization, Chinese alchemy was primarily concerned with the finding of the Elixir of Immortality—again, either at the lower level of prolonging physical life for its own sake, or for finding personal immortality, or, on the spiritual side, prolonging life in this world in order to gain more time to spiritualize the soul or to gain immortality as the enlightened being, the 'True Man' at one with the Tao.

The Chinese approach was through the fundamental doctrine of *yin* and *yang;* the influence of, and dependence on, the *I Ching,* the Book of Changes; and the teaching of the Five Elements School of thought, the whole outlook being more on a mental-spiritual level, even in its lower branches, than the gold-seeking slant of western alchemy. Materialism came later as a decadent growth in Chinese alchemy at certain periods; but, as Waley says, the work with metals and elixirs had practically ceased by AD 1000 and given place to the mystical path, which still used alchemical phraseology and symbolism. Of this stage he says that: 'Whereas in reading the works of western alchemists one constantly suspects that the quest with which they are concerned is a purely spiritual one; that they are using romantic phraseology of alchemy merely to poeticize religious experience, in China there is no such disguise. Alchemy becomes there openly and avowedly what it almost seems to be in the works of Böehme or Thomas Vaughan.' Chinese alchemy, with its emphasis on longevity and immortality, is much easier to account for than that of the West. Serious western scholars and alchemists often had to cover their spiritual quest with the trappings of the laboratory and the search for material gold for fear of persecution as heretics; but the Chinese searcher after the Tao could reasonably study and follow experiments in which he 'spiritualized' himself: he did not need to make concessions to the material gold cult. A further difference between East and West lay in the theistic attitudes adopted in the Work. The western alchemist, if he were involved in the esoteric, spiritual branch of the Work, invoked the God of monotheism. His eastern counterpart in classical Taoism was non-theistic, living in accord with and working for Nature and the impersonal Tao and calling on no god; but the 'bellows blowers,' as the exoteric, personal seekers were called, invoked a host of gods, spiritual beings and powers and were closely involved with spirits and demons, repelling the latter and depending on the aid of benevolent spirits.

There is no doubt at all that alchemy operated in two distinct branches existing side by side: the physical and the metaphysical. The true alchemy was the realm of the mystic, its aim being the transmutation of base man into perfection; but at the same time there existed the materialistically motivated gold seekers together with the seriously scientifically-minded knowledge seekers and experimentalists, of whom Paracelsus said: 'They do not give themselves up to ease and idleness . . . but they devote themselves diligently to their labours, sweating whole nights over fiery furnaces. These do not kill time with empty talk, but find delight in their laboratory.'[1]

Chinese alchemy, embedded in Taoism, was probably mystical in character before it became a science or art; it was sacred before it became profane, so that in a sense the scientific-chemical aspect was a decadent stage. The two branches could have little in the way of contact or mutual understanding, since the esoteric, mystical side could engender no desires, for these do not exist in the Tao; the reverse was true of the gold, or elixir, or longevity seekers. Ko Hung, in the *Pao P'u Tzu*, wrote that the adept in Taoism regards 'a peerage as an execution cauldron, a seal of office as a mourning dress, gold and jade as dirt, a splendid hall as a prison. How different from those pseudo-alchemists who, clenching their fists, mouth empty phrases and wait for good luck, or who lead a leisurely life in a gorgeous room, endowed with countless grants, appointed to high office, and still are discontented with their power and wealth!'

The Chinese made a crucial distinction between external, inorganic, laboratory alchemy and the internal, philosophical side; the former was concerned with the Elixir, or Pill, of Immortality, with ingredients and recipes using minerals or plants, a work which incidentally gave rise to the experimental, metallurgic, chemical and material aspects; the latter, which operated within the adept's own body and soul, was concerned with the psychological and spiritual side, with immortality and the spiritual transformation into the True Man. The one was the exoteric 'outer elixir,' in Chinese the *wei tan*; the other the 'inner elixir,' the esoteric *nei tan*; the one was material, the other spiritual. Laboratory alchemy, dealing with material experiments, was quantitative; the inner alchemy, striving towards spiritual perfection, was qualitative. For the spiritual work, the outward and exoteric aspect was merely a symbol of the inner work.

On the lowest level were those motivated by greed and hope of gain, either of material wealth or psychic powers; those who mistook the real work of spiritual gold for material riches. These were known in Chinese alchemy as the 'bellows blowers' or 'puffers;' in the West they were called 'charcoal burners,' 'bunglers,' or 'messy cooks.' There were also the charlatans who battened on the greed or credulity of emperors, princes, or the public. Some promised great results, or claimed to know of some place where the required minerals could be found, persuading princes and patrons to equip them with the money and necessities for the journey, and then disappearing. However, even here, on the lower level, experiments could lead to knowledge of the properties of the metals and herbs used in the processes and gave birth to early metallurgy and chemistry, while genuine experimentalists arrived at an understanding that was sometimes in advance of present-day scientific achievement.

The Taoism from which alchemy arose had as its main teaching that humanity should learn to live in harmony with Nature, with the Tao. Those who achieved this harmony did so through a spiritual-mystical understanding of the universe and its laws. The achievement naturally led to a balanced outlook, an acceptance of Nature's way, and therefore to a relaxed and happy temperament that was naturally conducive to good health through lack of stress and strain. Others, the less discerning, who saw the results but were either incapable of or unwilling to follow the Way, might assume that the mystic had some hidden secret of success or long life and so might look for short cuts in drugs, recipes and elixirs—an attitude still evident today in those who seek spiritual or psychic experiences through the medium of drugs: the lower alchemy.

This lower alchemy appealed to all the least desirable qualities in human nature: greed of gold, envy, unhealthy curiosity, vanity. The true alchemy led to the exact opposite, the recognition of the need for improvement in oneself and the lot of others; it was the 'hidden work' which humbly sought for illumination and the transmutation of the base leaden qualities into the gold of the True Man, a work carried out away from any publicity in the solitariness of one's own soul. In the West, societies allied to alchemy, such as masonry and rosicrucianism, were also insistent that the majority misunderstood the true work and taught that: 'Moreover the object of our guiltless guild is not the making of gold ... Rather we remove the erroneous opinion from them [the disciples] in so far as they are infected with it, even on the first steps to the temple of wisdom. They are earnestly enjoined against these errors that they must seek the Kingdom of God and his righteousness.'[2]

The Taoist aim was to become the True Man (*chen jen*), 'true' in the sense of purified—in alchemical terms, ridding oneself of the dross of the base metals, which then become' true.' The True Man is beyond the *hsien*; he is the fully realized individual who has attained enlightenment and is beyond the need for, or the idea of, 'powers' and personal immortality.

3

HSIEN

Running through popular Chinese alchemy was the belief that it was possible to attain a bodily immortality; that the body could be so rarefied that it took on the attributes and possibilities of a spirit. It was not merely a matter of arresting the normal processes of ageing and decay but, through a lifetime of practices, creating a new subtle body, capable of 'flying on the wind,' of being in more than one place at once, immune from harm from fire, water or weapons and able to assume invisibility; in fact having all the supernatural powers.

To achieve this was to become a *hsien*. The word is usually translated as Immortal or Genie, but neither takes on the whole meaning, so the term is best left untranslated. As Giles says, it is 'a word which in its written form is a character composed of two pictographic elements, "man" and "mountain," thus it appeared that the name was originally applied to men who had retired from the world in order to live a hermit's life in the mountains. Their activities were mostly confined to the gathering of certain herbs and roots which, when eaten, would not only cure disease but also rejuvenate the body and lengthen its life beyond the normal span.' Though, for the most part *hsien* were associated with the mountains, there were also *hsien* of the sea connected with the remote Isles where the Immortals dwell and where the herb of immortality grows. But as Ko Hung says: 'They simply make their abodes wherever they prefer.'

Supernatural powers also developed as a result of these experiments with herbs and fungi—powers of transformation, passing through solids of fire, walking on water, and so on. The reasoning behind the cult was that if one became sufficiently in accord with the Tao, which was eternal, it should be possible to become one with this immortality. The material body was to be refined away gradually, made more and more subtle by diet, breathing and other yogic exercises until it became wholly etherealized. Nor is this belief dead, for John Blofeld, in his travels in modern but pre-communist China, met a Taoist recluse in a monastery, a highly erudite man, who was seriously intending to transmogrify his body into a 'shining, adamantine substance, weightless yet hard as jade.'

The powers of the *hsien* parallel those of the Theravadin Buddhist disciplines as set out in the *Satipatthana Sutra;* that is, that the yogin will attain the ability to become invisible, or to 'become many,' i.e., appear in several places at once, to penetrate solids, fly through the air, walk on water or plunge into the earth. Other acquisitions are the 'heavenly ear,' that is, being able to hear both terrestrial and celestial sounds, near or far off, and being able to see into other people's minds. These powers were, naturally, used in an entirely benevolent way for the good of humanity as well as for the *hsien* him or herself. This ability to transcend the elements was used by the *hsien* not only in daily life but also in alchemical work; the earth yielded its secrets to him and the powers of travelling in supernatural realms conferred a knowledge of life and death and abolished all fear of death.

The techniques for achieving *hsien*-hood all aimed at eliminating the factors which caused disruption and degeneration in the individual. Diet, herbs or medicines, and exercises were all used for arresting the ageing process, while emotional and psychological control and the cultivation of ease of mind and peace of spirit would confer freedom from the destructive tensions of life. Once physical and mental balance and harmony had been attained the disease-inducing and wearing-out influences would be eliminated or slowed down. Above all, it was the ability to live in harmony with Nature that was the goal and means of attaining realization. Also, the *hsien* would be a true Taoist in refusing to take himself or life too seriously, believing with Chuang Tzu that 'I and the universe are one,' and that life and death were part of that one and therefore both equally acceptable. The light-hearted, gamin spirit of Taoism was seen in the poetry of Li Po, who was called the 'banished *hsien*' and who met a characteristically *hsien* end to his life by being borne heavenwards on the back of a whale!

There are, however, other positive qualities and attributes necessary for achieving the state of the *hsien*. This is illustrated in the story of the *hsien* Shao Chün, in the Han dynasty, who had found the secret of the elixir and was summoned to the presence of the Emperor who wanted to share it. Shao Chün told him:

> So long as your Majesty cannot make an end of pride and extravagance and renounce the allurements of the senses; while smiting and killing go on unchecked and the passions of joy and anger are not overcome; while in your dominion there are spirits that are not submissive and in the market place there are executions and bloodshed, the great secret of the celestial drug cannot be mastered.

Like all true *hsien* Shao Chün did not die a conventional death but disappeared from his coffin leaving only his clothes complete and fastened 'like the slough of a cicada,' having 'undergone voluntary transformation.' His connection with alchemy is shown in his further instructions to the Emperor to

> sacrifice to the Furnace and you will be able to summon up the spirits. Having summoned up the spirits you may transmute cinnabar into pure gold. When you have produced pure gold, make it into eating and drinking vessels, and you will prolong your span of life. If your span of life is prolonged, you may behold the *hsien* who live on the Island of P'eng-lai. When you have seen them and performed the sacrifices of Heaven and Earth, then you will become immortal. This is what happened to the Yellow Emperor.

Arthur Waley, commenting on this passage, suggests that the statement that having prolonged your life you may be able to see the *hsien* implies that *hsien* are only visible to those who have increased their span of life to something approaching the immortal; in other words, only like can see like. This type of homoeopathy also seems to hold in the recipes used in the *Ts'an T'ung Ch'i* where it says: 'The way to make oneself *a hsien* lies in the use of drugs of a nature similar to oneself . . . Things that are similar in nature go together, strange things cannot be reconciled.'

Ko Hung said: 'No man ever got fine grain without tilling the soil and no man can ever attain *hsien*-hood without diligence.' So there are endless passages giving the necessary preliminary qualities. One must be kind and affectionate, practise the Golden Rule, rejoice in the good fortune of others and sympathize with their suffering; utter no curse; regard other people's success or failure as one's own; avoid pride, vaunting oneself, or concealing evil intent with flattery. Harmful things are sadness and uneasiness, but also excess of joy; wasting time lying abed; lying down after a heavy meal; drunkenness; celibacy; getting breathless after running; shouts of joy or weeping; long conversations and telling pointless stories; in short, there must be no excess. In a treatise on 'The Art of Acquiring a Long and Healthy Life' (the *Pen Ts'ao Kang Mu*), four rules are laid down: one must 'regulate the affections of the heart; be moderate in the use of food and drink; carry out the day's work to a system and plan; rest and sleep to certain definite rules.' In censuring the luxurious hunting lifestyle of princes and potentates, Ko Hung said that in contradistinction 'methods leading to *hsien*-hood . . . depend on extending love to all things that creep and crawl, so that nothing that breathes may be harmed.' This love should be extended 'to the very frontiers of the universe and to view others as we do ourselves.' He also said that two Emperors, Shih Huang Ti, who founded the Chin dynasty, and Wu Ti of the Han, both of whom encouraged alchemists and sought to find immortality and the Isles of the Blessed, 'had a hollow reputation for wanting *hsien*-hood, but they never experienced the reality of cultivating the divine process . . . wouldn't it be most unusual if they had managed to reject fine foods, neglect their desires, turn their backs on splendours and go forth alone in search of the silence of divinity and *hsien*-hood?' He added that 'those wishing to enter the path of geniehood are as numerous as the hairs on a buffalo, while the successful are as rare as the horn of the unicorn.'

Genghis Khan was said to have asked a venerable Taoist Immortal for the secret of longevity and was told that a pure heart and few desires were what was required. The Khan then said that the Venerable Master had been sent to awaken his conscience.

This insistence on moral rectitude, purification and noble qualities points to the fact that the alchemy involved was not a material matter; such attributes would not be necessary for the carrying out of merely chemical or laboratory experiments. That it was a spiritual quest is also made evident in the West by such statements and instructions as that of Basil Valentinus:

> First there should be the invocation of God, flowing from the depth of a pure and sincere heart, and a conscience which should be free from all hypocrisy and vice, and also from all cognate faults such as

arrogance, boldness, pride, luxury, worldly vanity, oppression of the poor and similar iniquities, which should be rooted out of the heart . . . that when a man appears before the Throne of God, to regain the health of his body, he may come with a conscience weeded of all tares, and be changed into a pure temple of God cleansed of all that defiles.

There were distinct grades of *hsien*. The lowest was the 'corpse free,' whose body disappeared at death or vanished after being placed in a coffin, which when examined later was usually found to contain only the clothes or identifying objects such as shoes, a sword, a bamboo staff or a bamboo tablet with red writing on it. One *hsien* disappeared from his usual haunts but left a bamboo effigy to be buried in his place. An ancient writing says: 'After the death of an adept seeking immortality, the form of the skeleton may remain behind while the Immortal goes away; that is what is meant by "corpse free" (*shih chieh*). When one is ready to rise up as an immortal, one leaves behind the malodorous house of clay, hence the expression "corpse" *(shih)* from which the *hsien* is liberated.' This stage is the *shih chieh hsien*.

The second grade was the *ti hsien* or earthly immortal, who, having achieved *hsien*-hood, chose to remain in an earthly environment and who 'resorted to a famous mountain.' The body became so refined that the *ti hsien* lived a life of the spirit, wandering amidst the beauties of the world and consorting with the like-minded.

The highest was the *t'ien hsien*, the heavenly or celestial immortal who ascended to heaven, rose to 'the aery void' and joined the supernatural spirits.

It was said that some remained in the first state of *shih chieh hsien* from choice. Such was the *hsien* Mr. White-stone, who was 2000 years old but looked like a man of forty. He maintained that the joys of heaven were not superior to those of earth, because on earth one was greatly respected as a *hsien* and would be no better off in heaven. This sort of *hsien* was probably one who deliberately only took half a dose of the elixir; but if he wanted to change his state he could always take the other half and become a celestial immortal. There was also, again, the vague and little mentioned class of aquatic *hsien* who were of the *yin*, watery, nature and lived in the waters.

Most *hsien,* whose biographies appear in the *T'u Shu Chi Ch'eng,* which has the lives of more than a thousand such immortals recorded, made their final exit from the world in a spectacular manner. They were people from every walk of life and every type of person, male and female; from princes such as Liu An of the Han dynasty, to humble beggars; from high officials to peasants; but the manner of their departure followed the same patterns. Sometimes the 'death' was followed by an amazing revivification such as happened when a *hsien* had been deliberately killed by some ill-disposed person; but more usual was the spectacular ride heavenwards, for example, as already quoted, Li Po departing on a whale. He, no doubt in consonance with his gamin sense of humour, would choose so incongruous a mount to go heavenwards! Lao Tzu himself travelled to the West; one account says he was borne away on a yellow buffalo, another that he disappeared into the heavens in a chariot drawn by a black ox. Ma Shih Huang, who was a horse doctor in the Yellow Emperor's reign and who also treated an ailing dragon, was later taken up to heaven by the dragon. Lü Shang, after living 2000 years, was placed in his coffin by a son, but when the son set about performing the funeral rites the coffin was found to be empty except for a jade seal and six bamboo manuscript tablets.

The beautiful girl Kou-i Fu-jen, who became the mother of the Emperor Chao Ti, was a *hsien.* She was murdered but her body did not grow cold in death and emitted a wonderful fragrance. Later, her coffin was found to contain nothing but a silk slipper. Yü Tzu, on the other hand, never died; he climbed a mountain and was seen to take off heavenwards in broad daylight.

The powers exercised by the *hsien* are fully illustrated in the story of the Eight Immortals who visited the Prince Liu An, a noted patron of alchemists. They were refused admittance by the Prince's gatekeeper when they appeared as old men, so they immediately changed into boys of fifteen with black hair and peach-blossom cheeks; this so frightened the gatekeeper that he ran to Liu An who in turn hastened to greet his visitors without even pausing to put on his shoes. He conducted the Immortals indoors and established them on furnishings of silk, gold and jade and burned incense of 'a hundred ingredients harmoniously compounded.' The *hsien* then changed back into old men and the Prince took up the position of a disciple, facing North, with hands raised in salutation.

Introducing themselves the *hsien* said:

One of us can cause wind and rain by sitting down, can raise clouds and fog by standing up, can make rivers and lakes by drawing lines on the ground and can create mountains by piling up sand.

One of us can crumble heights and fill up deeps, can control the tiger and leopard, and can catch the dragon and the snake and can master gods and ghosts and make them serve him.

One of us can separate his form and change his appearance, can cause life by sitting down and death by standing up, can cover a complete army from sight and can turn broad daylight into darkness.

One of us can ride in space and walk on emptiness, can go into the sea and the deep, can go in and out through any partitions and can breathe a breath of one thousand miles.

One of us can go into the fire without being scorched, into water without getting wet, can be stabbed without being hurt, can be aimed at but never hit by an arrow and is not cold in freezing water and does not sweat in summer.

One of us can perform thousands of changes at will, can bring forth birds and animals, weeds and woods, in a moment, and can move mountains, heights and rivers.

One of us can prevent havoc, reclaim from dangers, dispel evils, do away with harmful things and can cause longevity.

One of us can boil mud to get gold, assay lead to get silver, can fuse the eight minerals of the alchemist into a liquid form from which pearls flow and can ride the dragon and harness the clouds to travel afloat in the Great Clearness.

They then offered gifts to Liu An who made obeisance and served wines and fruit to them with his own hands. The abilities of the *hsien* were tested and confirmed and the Prince was given the Book of Medicines. The elixir was made up, but Liu An did not take it until later, when a jealous courtier informed falsely against him. The courtier persuaded the Emperor that Liu An had plotted against him and the Emperor, believing the informer, sent to bring the Prince to justice. The eight *hsien* then said: 'You must go now, this is a heaven-sent message for you to depart.' They all went together to the mountain, Liu An took the medicine and they all made a ceremonial offering, burying gold in the earth; then all rose heavenwards in broad daylight. Liu An's dog and the chickens in the courtyard picked up some of the pills and were immediately transported to heaven with him.

A different version of Liu An' s end is that, when the Emperor ordered him to commit suicide, he simply disappeared, ascending to heaven complete with his family and all his domestic animals, who had all taken the elixir. The same happened with Huai-nan Tzu, who wrote a treatise on alchemy and was said to have discovered the elixir of immortality, which he took and at once ascended in broad daylight in the presence of witnesses. As he rose in the air he dropped the jar containing the rest of the pills, which were picked up by his dog and hens who all promptly rose to heaven after him, where their barking and crowing was heard. This disappearance of an adept heavenwards is a familiar event in other cultures; the translation of Elijah to heaven in a fiery chariot, for example, and the case of the patriarch Enoch, who 'walked with God and was not.'

There are endless accounts of the wonder-working powers of the *hsien*. One crossed the Yangtze river in flood by pointing his fan at it, whereupon the waters divided and left him a passage on dry ground. Another *hsien* ambled off in an old donkey cart, which, when followed, could not be overtaken by a galloping horse. There was also a Pied Piper among them who charmed away a plague of rats, and there are accounts of feasts at which the wine jar was inexhaustible and the meat and delicacies never gave out.

In his *Pao P'u Tzu*, Ko Hung describes the state of the *hsien*:

Now once we can mount into the empty air and tread upon the light, with the clouds as our vehicles and rainbows for canopies, we shall be able to taste the dews of roseate morning vapours and quaff the intoxicating essences of the deep blue heavens and the yellow earth. For drink we shall have nectar of jade and ambrose of gold, for food we shall taste cerulean iridescent mushrooms and vermilion-red flowers; our dwellings will be of jasper and sardine-stone, with rooms composed of rubescent gems; and we shall wander in the realm of Great Purity.

There is much in common with the traditional spirit and fairy world in the powers exhibited by the *hsien*—in their powers of invisibility, shape-shifting and flying, and in their ability to pass through solids and summon up the magic table that provides unlimited food and drink. There is also the phenomena of time-loss and timelessness, as in fairy stories, when mortals disappear for what seems a few moments or hours only to return and find a world hundreds of years older.

The *hsien* Tung-fang went missing for a year as a child; on being reproached by his foster-mother, he gave an account of wanderings in supernatural realms, though he insisted that he had gone out in the morning and returned at noon on the same day. Two friends who went into the mountains to collect herbs for recipes got lost for thirteen days but finally found a peach tree and ate its fruit and drank from a stream; they then came across two amazingly beautiful maidens and stayed in their magnificent abode for ten days, after which they decided it was time to return home. The fairy women had them escorted on their way with music and singing, but on reaching 'home' found that seven generations had passed, though they managed to find a descendant of the family who remembered the story of a distant ancestor who had disappeared into the mountains and never returned. Another *hsien*, Wang Chih, was given a date stone to suck when he went into the forest to cut wood. There he stayed for a short time with the fairies, but when he arrived back in the mortal world his axe-handle had crumbled to dust and several centuries had gone by.

The idea of the *hsien* greatly appealed to the Chinese mind and there were countless stories of the Immortals or Genii. But although legends and interest abounded, few actually undertook the work of transformation. A passage from a Sung dynasty treatise, on alchemical techniques, reads: 'As for the affairs of elixirs, chemicals and the furnaces, scholars, high-ranking ministers and learned Taoists, ensconced in mountain and forest retreats, all love talking about them and searching them out. I should think that seven or eight out of ten are like this, but I doubt whether all of them are bent upon getting the chemical medicines of immortality to become *hsien*.'

Not only were there the dilettantes, there were also the charlatans, the 'false teachers' against whom Ko Hung inveighed as those who 'utter clever and eloquent inanities.' He instances cases of false teachers and casts doubt on some of the accounts of *hsien* leaving empty coffins. He wrote of one pseudo-teacher who fooled many of his followers during his life and 'the crowd believed everything they heard of him,' while 'those of us who knew the stories he told treated them as a matter of laughter.' This false teacher grew old and forgetful (which a *hsien* should never do), fell ill and died. It was assumed that he had been transformed, but when a pupil, at whose home he had died, bored a hole in the coffin a year later, the corpse was still there.

That several *hsien* were executed by emperors or killed by jealous or vicious enemies does not in any way imply lack of powers, either prophetic or magical, on their part for not avoiding such a fate. Execution was often regarded as a means of release from the body by the 'sword method,' and in such cases the *hsien* was always seen to be alive and well some days later, or the coffin found to be empty except for some identifying object. One such *hsien*, Kung-yüan, who was beheaded by the Emperor in a fit of fury, reappeared and told the Emperor that it was all a joke to him: 'One who has attained to *hsien*-hood is immune from all calamity. Heaven and Earth might be engulfed and still he would remain unscathed; how much less could he be injured by ordinary weapons.'

4

LONGEVITY AND IMMORTALITY

The desire for longevity, immortality and the conquest of death occurs in most civilizations, religions and mythologies, but is particularly prevalent in Chinese life and literature. In the conventional greeting of wishing 'long life, health, wealth and happiness,' it is the long life that is the most important and the character for longevity appears everywhere, stylized in literally dozens of ways in art, on talismans and ornaments. The Chinese having always had an extreme reverence for old age, the pictograph also stands for old age, 'enduring forever,' a long life and prosperity; but in the popular branch of Taoism its immortality aspect can also signify death, with a religious immortality meaning.

Some idea of the extent of the longevity aimed at in alchemy may be given by the story of Huang An, who preserved his body by eating cinnabar. He sat on the back of a tortoise for so long that its shell became quite flat. When asked how long he had been there he replied: 'The tortoise fears the light of the sun and the moon and puts its head out only once in 2000 years. This I have seen it do five times already since I have been sitting here.' When he was wandering about instead of sitting he carried the tortoise on his back.

In the classical Taoism of Chuang Tzu this prolongation of life was not advocated. He wrote: 'How do I know that loving life is not a delusion? How do I know that by hating death I am not one who, having left his home in his youth, has forgotten the way back? . . . How do I know that the dead do not wonder why they have ever longed for life?' He also said that 'What makes my life good makes death good . . . the Sage delights in early death, he delights in old age; he delights in the beginning; he delights in the end,' and 'The True Man of ancient times knew nothing of loving life and hating death. He who clearly apprehends the scheme of existence, does not rejoice over life nor repine at death, for he knows that these are not final.'

There is no doubt, though, that in alchemy the long life of the body played an important part. At one level the cult of longevity had the objective of prolonging life in the body for the sake of gaining more time for the development of the spirit. This attitude also occurs in Indian and Tantric alchemy. There are accounts of Indian yogins living for more than three hundred and fifty years. The theme also appears in Muslim writings, probably having been spread westward from China via Turkistan.

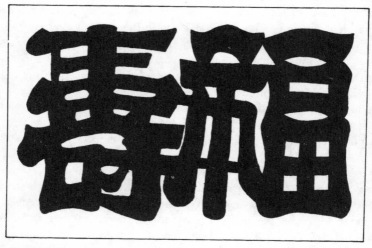

Talismanic characters for Longevity and Happiness

As to immortality, 'The body must be brought into complete subjection to, and into complete harmony with, the principles of the Tao. Through this process the body would eventually acquire the attributes of the Tao, and since Tao is immortal, immortality of the body would be a natural and logical result. Death would not ensue, for after the complete process of acquiring Tao, the physical essence of the human organism would become refined and might no longer be distinguished from the spiritual essence. Through the agency of Tao, therefore, man might become, truly and completely, an immortal being.' O. S. Johnson, from whose study of Chinese alchemy this passage is quoted, sees in this stage of the development of Taoist thought the crucial transition period from the classical, philosophical Taoism of Lao Tzu and Chuang Tzu to a utilitarian and popular religion, having in it the seeds of Chinese alchemy.

Chinese religion and philosophy did not have the otherworldly outlook of the Mesopotamian-Mediterranean beliefs, since in Chinese thought spirit and matter were not sharply divided; both were held to operate together in the world of Nature, so when the body had been sufficiently purified and etherealized it could continue to exist in this world, or in the heavens, or both. Thus, having reached this state, some of the Immortals ascended to heaven while others chose to remain on earth. In the Mesopotamian-Mediterranean religions this conquest of death took the form of the perennial theme in mythology of the cult of the Dying God who dies only to come to life again; such are Osiris, Dionysos, Attis, Odin and all the messiahs and culture heroes.

In the *Pao P'u Tzu*, Ko Hung argues the case for immortality from observations of metempsychosis: 'Creatures which fly and run, and creatures which crawl, all derive a fixed form from the Foundation of Change. Yet suddenly they may change the old body and become totally different things. Of those changes there are so many thousands and tens of thousands that one could never come to the end of detailing them.' In his autobiography he also argues that:

> The shallow-minded ... merely say that because they see no genii in their world it is not possible that such things exist But what is so special about what our eyes have seen? Why should there be any limit to the numbers of marvellous things that exist between sky and earth, within the vastness of the Unbounded? All our lives we have a sky over our heads but never know what is above it; to the end of our days we walk the earth without ever seeing what is below it. Our bodies are our very own, but we never come to understand how our hearts and wills become what they are. An allotment of life is ours, but we never understand how its actual measure is achieved; and this is even more true in the case of the more abstruse patterns governing gods and genii ... isn't it a sad spectacle to see people relying upon the surface perceptions of eyes and ears in judging the existence of the subtle and the marvellous?

The famous Eight Immortals or Genii, the most celebrated of all the *hsien*, seem to be a later form of the Eight Worthies of the Early Han dynasty, since they do not appear until the thirteenth century, though most of its members are associated with the T'ang dynasty. They are

The Eight Immortals crossing the sea.

immensely popular figures in Chinese art, being portrayed in every medium: painting, embroidery, scrolls, fans, jade and wood carvings, on vases and all ceramics. They represent a complete cross-section of the people, as has been said, male and female, rich and poor, old and young, military and scholarly, noble and peasant and they also cover a wide historical range, though only three of them can be identified as historical figures; the others are the stuff of legend and fable, 'wild history;' but all are subjects of a huge volume of romance, legend and popular veneration. They are said to be 'the embodiment of the ideas of perfect but imaginary happiness which possess the minds of the Chinese people.'

The earliest, said to be the founder of the group, was Chung-li Ch'üan. He was reputed to have been a Han marshal, but there is no historical evidence for this. His birth was accompanied, traditionally, by various marvellous phenomena. He was converted to the Tao by an aged man and left his rank and profession to become a wanderer. He became an alchemist, transmuted metals into silver in a time of famine and distributed it among the poor, so saving many lives. The secret of immortality was revealed to him while meditating; a stone wall broke and revealed a jade casket containing the secret. After following the instructions his room was filled with rainbow clouds and music; a crane then came to carry him heavenwards. During his journeyings he met the Taoist adept T'ao Hung-ching, who gave him 'a pinch of the Great Monad,' a fire-charm and some spiritual elixir. (The Great Monad is the Tao, the cosmic force that pre-exists the manifest world.) Chung-li Ch'üan's attributes are a feathered fan and a flywhisk, or sometimes a two-edged sword and the peach of immortality. He is depicted as a fat and bearded old man scantily clad.

Chang Kuo was a hermit who rode a miraculous white donkey that could cover immense distances in a day. Sometimes he rode facing the head, sometimes the tail of the donkey. When Chang Kuo dismounted he folded the donkey up like paper and put it away; when he wanted it again he sprayed water over it from his mouth and it became a donkey once more. Various emperors tried to lure the adept to the court, but he refused all invitations, even to marry an Imperial Princess, until the final one from the Empress Wu Tse T'ien. He went to court, lay down and died; but this was only a ruse for escaping from imperial importunities. His body was seen to decompose (a different version of the empty-coffin theme), but this, too, was a trick as he was seen alive and well in the mountains a short time afterwards. He is portrayed seated on his donkey and holding a fish-drum and castanets or a phoenix feather.

Lü Yen, or Lü Tung-pin, was a scholar of the T'ang dynasty who came from an official family; in spite of failing his degree he became a patron of literature. He had a dream of future success, high office and glory followed by disgrace, exile and misery, so he renounced worldly ambition and retired to the mountains. He met, and became a pupil of, Chung-Ii Ch'üan and was tested by ordeals and a host of demons. He experienced the time-illusion when cooking some millet, dreaming a life-time of history; but on waking he found the millet still uncooked. He is depicted as a scholar and his attribute is a magic two-edged sword which conferred invisibility and with which he defeated demons. He founded the tradition of the Elixir of Life which is associated with the T'ang dynasty, during which it was developed but kept esoteric. Lü Yen claimed that he obtained his knowledge from the Master of the Pass, Kuan Yin-hsi, the man who had asked Lao Tzu to write down his wisdom before disappearing over the Pass to the West. This was the traditional origin of the *Tao Tê Ching*.

Li T'ieh-kuei, 'Li with the staff,' is portrayed as an ugly beggar, leaning on a crutch. Originally an imposing and handsome man, he left his body behind when he went off in spirit to meet Lao Tzu in a sacred mountain. One story is that he was gone so long that a disciple had his body cremated. Another version is that he left instructions for his body to be cremated after seven days; on the sixth day the disciple who was looking after the body had news that his mother had died and, feeling sure that Li would not return, cremated the body. Returning on the seventh day, Li's spirit saw only a heap of ashes, and so he entered the body of a beggar who had just died by the roadside. He then lived on in the disguise of a crippled beggar, leaning on a staff. He is often accompanied by a crane of immortality and has a gourd-bottle from which a vapour (his spirit) rises; he used to hang the gourd up at night and jump into it and stay there till morning. After entering the beggar's body Li went to the disciple's house and stopped the preparations for the mother's funeral by restoring her to life.

One version of his departure from the world was that he changed into a dragon and ascended heavenwards; another was that he told a disciple that if he stepped on a leaf floating on the water it would bear

The Immortal Wnag-tzu Ch'iao playing the *sheng* while riding through the clouds on a crane.

him safely. The disciple refused, whereupon Li said he was obviously too heavy with the cares of the world and then stepped on the leaf himself and vanished.

Han Hsiang Tzu was a nephew of the renowned T'ang poet Han Yü. He was born with all the marks of a *hsien* and devoted himself to alchemy and to finding the elixir. He was killed falling from the Peach Tree of Immortality, which he had climbed in an attempt to pluck the fruit. He was immediately transfigured and then reappeared as a Taoist priest. His attributes are a flute, castanets and the alchemist's crucible.

Lan Ts'ai-ho appears as either a good-looking but unkempt youth or as a girl whose life was spent in wine taverns as a flautist and singer, giving away the money earned to the poor and sleeping in the snow in winter. When depicted as a girl her breath rises in brilliant colours. She wrote poetry condemning the delusions of the world's pleasures and ended by soaring up to heaven from a wine tavern on the back of a crane, her dress, belt and castanets falling to earth. Attributes are a basket of flowers associated with immortality, such as the plum or peach blossom, chrysanthemums, the pine and bamboo.

Ho Hsien Ku was a girl of fourteen or fifteen when she was visited by a divinity who gave her powdered mica to eat to etherealize her body. She also experienced the time-illusion when she was given a peach to eat and found she had been away for a month instead of a day, as she had supposed; she had gone without food all that time with no ill effects.

Afterwards she lived on a rainbow powder made from oystershells and moonbeams and returned to the mountains, flying backwards and forwards from her home like a bird, finally ascending to heaven in broad daylight. Her attribute is the bamboo ladle she was using in the kitchen at the time when she was translated. Her story has Cinderella-and-stepmother nuances.

That the *hsien* could be translated to the land of the immortals without going through the experience of physical death assumed the existence of that land, an assumption not confined to China but prevalent the world over in the belief in Paradise, the Isles of the Blessed, the Abode of Song, the Green Isle and the Elysian Fields to give a few of its names.

There were various paradises in Chinese mythology: for the earthly *hsien* there was the Earthly Paradise; an account of this is given when

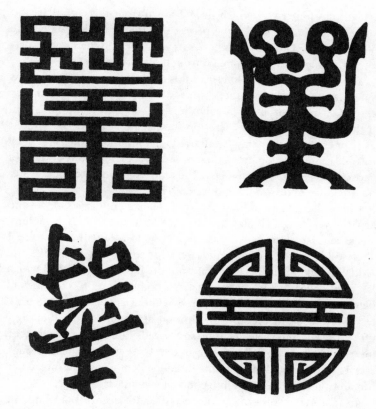

Styles of the Longevity character

Yü the Great lost his way and 'came to a country which lay on the North shore of the Northern Ocean . . . it was called "Northernland" and we don't know what lay on its boundaries. There was neither wind nor rain there, neither frost nor snow. It did not produce birds, animals, insects, fishes, plants and trees the same as ours. All around it seemed to rise into the sky.' In the centre of this land there was a mountain from which streams of water flowed continually. 'This was called "Divine Spring." The perfume of the water was more delicious than that of orchids or pepper, and its taste was better than that of wine or ale. The spring divided into four rivers which flowed down from the mountain and watered the whole land . . . the people were gentle, following Nature without wrangling or strife; their hearts were soft and their bodies delicate; arrogance and envy were far from them.'

The Yellow Emperor also visited this realm in a dream. It was 'tens of thousands of miles distant . . . it was beyond the reach of ships or vehicles or any mortal foot. Only the soul could travel so far.' As in Yü the Great's Paradise, so here too the people were gentle 'without desire or cravings; they simply followed their natural instincts . . . They bestrode the air as though treading on solid earth; they were cradled in space as though resting on a bed. They moved about like gods. Water had no power to drown them nor fire to hurt them.'

China also had a tradition of a grey, shadowy underworld, beyond the Yellow Springs, similar to the place known to the Babylonians, Greeks and Israelites, but it was not a popular belief. The most usual otherworld was the Western Paradise, a concept shared by Taoists and Buddhists alike. This was different from the Earthly Paradise in which the *hsien* could live in his etherealized body among the beauties of the earth, or wander among the stars without contact with the ordinary world of humanity. But the Immortal could also dwell entirely in the heavens and the stars, if he so desired. Taoist otherworld ideas, however, differed from Buddhism in that there were no hells, though later Taoism adopted many of the Buddhist demons which threatened humanity and frightened it into good behaviour.

In Taoism the Western Paradise was presided over by Hsi Wang Mu, Queen of Heaven; in Buddhism the Amida Buddha resided in the Pure Land: both had a Peach as the Tree of Life growing in the centre and both were the dwelling place of Immortals, Genii and fairies as well as those souls who by virtue had won entrance to Paradise. Both these concepts were a popular degeneration from the original non-theistic metaphysics of the impersonal Tao and the equally impersonal Nirvana; both were based on the notion of materialistic reward, the one for successful adherence to the rules of physical and spiritual discipline, the other for faith and calling on the Name. The Western Paradise was paved with gold, silver and jade, pearls and crystal. The seven lakes were fringed by golden sand and there were beautiful pavilions of translucent jewels; beautiful birds sang and flowers were full of colour and fragrance.

Candelabrum with stylized Longevity and Happiness characters.

There are also traditions and records going back to the third century BC of Emperors sending expeditions to search for the Palace of the Immortals, which was believed to be situated in the mountains of northern Tibet. The dwellers in this region lived in both worlds at once, the natural and the spiritual. Here we have an echo of the theme of Shangri-la. Ssu-ma Ch'ien, the great historian (163-85 BC) wrote of these Mountains of the Immortals as being the Land of the Blessed where the elixir is found and where all things are white and the palaces are gold and silver.

While the *hsien* could live either in the earthly or celestial realm, the real goal of the alchemist was to reach the Isles of the Immortals, the

Fairy Isles where the herb of immortality grew. These floating isles—five originally—were reputed to be situated a great way off in the Po Sea, to the East of China. One of the gods arranged for fifteen huge turtles, in relays of five, to hold up the islands on their heads. This arrangement was maintained until a great giant, who wanted their shells for divination, fished for and caught six of the turtles, whereupon two of the islands floated away to the North Pole and sank into the ocean. The Immortals living on those islands had to move to the three that remained; there they cultivated the herb of immortality. These were the Isles of P'eng-lai, Fang-chan and Ying Chou, the most frequently mentioned being P'eng-lai. All living things, birds, animals and plants are perfectly white (symbolic of the white and vitality of quicksilver), and the palaces and gates are made of gold and jewels, silver and pearls. If you see the Isles from a distance they look like clouds, but when you get near them they sink into the sea and a wind suddenly blows you away from them. The food there is miraculous and fruits if eaten will preserve the eater from old age and death. This, again, is reminiscent of the Peach of Immortality growing in the Western Paradise and of the Tree of Life in all paradisial mythology.

One of the people greatly interested in finding these Isles was Shih Huang Ti (259-210 BC), founder of the Ch'in dynasty and the first real Emperor of China, who unified the country after the period of the Warring States, making it an Empire instead of a collection of smaller kingdoms and states. It was he who built the Great Wall to keep out the northern barbarians; he introduced the hair-brush, or pencil, for writing or drawing on silk instead of the bamboo tablets used before; but he also achieved notoriety in his 'burning of the books,' ordering the destruction of the Confucian Classics, which he maintained were receiving an exaggerated reverence and were stultifying scholarship. He was greatly interested in alchemy and in his reign appeared the famous alchemists An Ch'i Sheng and Hsü Fu or Hsü She. The former, a vague legendary character, was believed to be a thousand years old; he was highly learned, especially in compounding medicines. He so impressed Shih Huang Ti that the Emperor continued talking to him for three days and nights, finally presenting the Sage with much gold and jade, in which, as a true Taoist, he saw no value so threw it away. He was said to live on a pill as large as a melon.

Ssu-ma Ch'ien records in his *History* that Hsü Fu was sent on an expedition (some say he went at his own request, others that it was the Emperor's wish) to find the Isles of the Immortals and bring back the elixir of immortality. Shih Huang Ti equipped the expedition with the 'five grains' and Hsu set out with three thousand youths and maidens, and artisans and workmen of all kinds. The expedition never returned. Some believed that they had found the Isles; another tradition said that Hsü Fu discovered the islands of peace and plenty and settled there and became king of the new realm; others suggest that this was the discovery of the Japanese Islands. Shih Huang Ti always hoped that the expedition would return and used to go to the coast, wandering up and down it, gazing out to sea, searching the horizon for the returning ships.

The Emperor Wu, of the Han dynasty, a great believer in alchemy and astrology, also sent an expedition to the island of P'eng-lai to bring back the elixir; but it too failed to come back. During his reign various alchemists made claims that they had discovered the secret of immortality and transmuting metals, but, failing to produce results, were executed. The Emperor finally came to the conclusion that he had been led astray by the extravagant claims of the magicians and decided that 'if we are temperate in our diet and use medicine, we make our illnesses few. That is all we can attain to.'

While Shih Huang Ti and Wu Ti (the word *Ti* means Emperor) and other alchemists took the existence of the Isles literally, they were, from the esoteric aspect, an allegory of the attainment of the state of enlightenment, the inner world of spirit for which the adept worked; a state of being rather than a 'place;' the mystical states in which spiritual knowledge is achieved and it is realized that there is no death.

5

THE ELIXIR

The Elixir, the Golden Pill or the Pill of Immortality was for the East what the Philosophers' Stone was for western alchemy; both are ill-defined but were basically a substance of which a small portion could transform a much larger quantity of base metals into gold, or could confer immortality. Both had the property of transforming one thing into another, both could cure diseases and restore youth; the same phraseology is used to describe either. Many a Taoist account tells of the restoration of youthfulness, or grey hair turning black, and of a man of a hundred years old looking as if he were in the prime of his life. In the West, Solomon Trismosin said that by taking a grain of the stone his wrinkled skin became smooth and white, his cheeks rosy, his grey hair black and his bowed back erect. He also said he restored youthfulness to ninety-year-old ladies and that the stone was a universal panacea.

All sorts of extravagant claims were made for the transmuting powers of the elixir and the stone. Ma Hsiang, a *hsien,* always paid for his wine by turning all the iron vessels in the wine shop into gold. Albertus Magnus was reported to have brought to life a bronze statue made by Thomas Aquinas, who made use of it as a servant; unfortunately, it was somewhat talkative and noisy and had to be kept in order with a hammer.

There is, however, a sharp division between the aims of the exoteric 'bellows blower' or 'charcoal burner' and the esoteric searcher for wisdom and enlightenment, and the elixir itself was named in various categories as exoteric or esoteric: the 'inner elixir', the *nei tan,* of meditation and spiritual practices developed the qualities of the soul and was the esoteric aspect; the 'outer elixir', the *wei tan,* of taking medicines, herbs and the pill of immortality was the exoteric side intended to bring about physical regeneration. There were also the *hsien tan* of the Immortals and the divine elixir, *shen tan.*

With the deliberately esoteric nature of alchemy it followed that instructions and recipes were not made available to the general public or the merely curious, so most of the methods of concocting the elixir are not known and even of those specifically mentioned many are not now identifiable. Also, when the exact ingredients are given, the proportions are withheld, so that, for example, when the famous 'eight precious things' of the elixir are given as cinnabar, realgar, sulphur, orpiment, saltpetre, ore of cobalt, salt and mica, no measures are included. In addition to this difficulty there were widely differing local and dynastic weights and measures. Then, too, the methods of concocting the elixir are couched in obscure terms using names which are deliberately esoteric, if not at times deliberately misleading, so that it is now impossible to follow either the ancient recipes or the exact physical techniques. What Jung said about western alchemy applies equally to the Chinese science: 'It is quite hopeless to try to establish any kind of order in the infinite chaos of substances and procedures. Seldom do we get even an approximate idea of how the work was done, what materials were used, and what results achieved. The reader usually finds himself in the most impenetrable darkness when it comes to names and substances; they could mean almost anything.' In any case, as cannot be too frequently stressed, they were not intended to mean anything to the uninitiated and were only for transmission from a master to a pupil with whom such dangerous secrets could be trusted. 'The vulgar and debased cannot practise this art, neither such as have no understanding,' as Ko Hung said in his *Pao P'u Tzu*.

Recipes for the elixir *(tan)* are endless, literally in hundreds. As Professor Needham says of Chinese science and alchemy, it is a matter of 'finding the way successfully through an incohate mass of ideas, and the facts so hard to establish, relating to alchemy and metallurgy in ancient, medieval and traditional China.' Also, 'there is a veritable ocean, only a small part of which has been explored.' It is also a question of separating the grains of wheat from the mass of chaff of the 'bellows blowers.' Even if recipes are specific, it is not always known what is meant by substances with such fanciful names as Scarlet Snow, the Flowing Pearl Elixir, the Empyrean-Roaming Elixir, the Pale Moon Elixir, and so on; but all of them guarantee immortality. Ko Hung says that such elixirs are not intended to be generally known, so does not give methods of preparation and the uninitiated would do well to leave it at that. Ingredients for the Empyrean-Roaming Elixir are: cinnabar, realgar, malachite, laminar, amorphous sulphur and quicksilver. It is known that the Flowing Pearl is an esoteric name for quicksilver. On the other hand, some recipes were clearly given and even the exact places from which the ingredients were to be collected were specified; 'all others are best rejected.'

The reputation of the crane for longevity made it a symbol of immortality; it was also a messenger between gods and men, hence its eggs were an appropriate food for those seeking immortality and contact with supernatural beings. The cock, as a *yang* bird, supplied vital force in its comb, which was used in recipes, while the hen provided the *yin* balancing force in its eggs. The tortoise, which is one of the four 'spiritually endowed creatures' and extremely long-lived, symbolized both longevity and strength, so that a preparation made from tortoise shells can confer one thousand years of life.

There are such recipes as taking a swan's egg, sealed with lacquer, and steeped in a mica solution. After one hundred days it will turn red: a gill of this will increase your life by a hundred years, or a quart by a thousand. Another prescription says: 'Prepare three pounds of the skin and fat from the back of a hog and one quart of strong vinegar. Place five ounces of yellow gold in a container and cook in an earthen stove. Dip the gold in and out of the fat one hundred times; likewise in the vinegar. Take a pound of this and you will outlast all nature; half a pound and you will live two thousand years.'

Other elixirs will even raise the dead, others will confer 'everlasting vision' and so etherealize the body that 'in full sun you will cast no shadow.' In many cases strange and grotesque ingredients are required, such as black dung from a black cow, black insects' blood, seeds of red fir, dragons' grease, ox gall, earthworm excreta; many of these, of course, would be a disguise. Equally strange ingredients were used in western alchemy: the urine of a dog, the hairs of a white dog; the blood of a mouse, asses' dung; while pearls and stones found in a crab's head are specifics against heart trouble; a contraceptive is to bind the head with a red ribbon or hold a stone found in the head of an ass, and baldness can be cured by the application of bees burned to ashes.

Another recipe guarantees that 'having eaten the medicine for three years a man attains buoyancy of movement and is able to travel great distances; stepping over fire, he is not scorched; dropped into water, he does not get wet. He is able to appear and disappear at will. He will be happy for ever.'

Careful preparation is necessary before attempting the work of making the elixir. In the first place, both eastern and western alchemy depended on astrology in calculating the propitious times and seasons for experiments and for compounding medicines and the elixir. Then the alchemical work required abstinence from certain foods, notably cereals and meat, for one hundred days, and a ritual purification which involved the use of perfumes in washing the body and hair. The preparations should be carried out in an uninhabited place, usually a sacred mountain. This need for solitude in the work is insisted on universally; it was a *sine qua non* for success. In China it was the retreat to the mountain; in India to the forest 'far away from all unclean presence;' in Babylon the alchemist had to work alone, 'a stranger shall not enter,' while in the West the same applied to the alchemist in his laboratory. Ko Hung attributed the failure of the earlier alchemists, employed by the Emperor Wu, in making gold and finding the elixir to the fact that they attempted the work in the palace and at court instead of the solitary retreat in the mountains.

It is necessary to pay reverence to, and invoke, the proper divinities and powers; to have faith and to be blest by being born under the right stars. These ritual preparations, and the condition that only initiates or disciples are present during the work, are evident in all branches of alchemy. 'Common people or anything that soils' must be avoided and no disbelievers may be told of the plans, for, if they blaspheme the divine medicine, the preparation will not be successful. It is also necessary to avoid any possibility of the evil eye. 'Even a doctor . . . will avoid being seen by fowls, dogs, children or women . . . lest his remedies lose their efficacy.' This last, however, is at variance with the vital help given by wives who had the necessary knowledge or 'fate' in cases where the man was unsuccessful in his experiments. The Yellow Emperor, for instance, was dependent on his Immortal maids and much of the work needed the help of the yin female balance; in the West this was given by the 'sister' in the work.

For the 'inner alchemy,' the esoteric side, to quote from the *Ts'an T'ung Ch'i*, 'Attention should be turned to the well-being of the inner self so as to attain the state of perfect calmness and freedom from matter. The primordial substance, shining forth unseen, will illuminate the insides of the body . . . Cessation of thought is desirable and worries are preposterous.' The concluding chapter of the work makes it clear that immortality in its true sense, not mere longevity, is to be achieved, for even a small quantity of the elixir is enough to 'confer tranquillity on the *hun p'o* [soul], give it immortality and enable it to live with the immortals.'

Chinese alchemy is full of accounts of the Pill of Immortality, which is one of its chief distinctions from the western branch with its emphasis on gold. The pill or elixir has, though, close associations with the Persian *haoma* and Indian *soma* in that they, like the elixir, also cured diseases as well as conferring immortality. According to the *Rig Veda*, to drink *soma* was to become immortal. There is also a connection with the sacred mushroom, the *peyotl* of the Mexicans. The cult of all these substances was based on the belief that it was possible to achieve immortality, either by the concoction of a drug, whether from mineral, plant or animal sources, which could both rejuvenate and preserve the physical body, which became so refined that it developed the qualities of the *hsien;* or, alternatively, to reach the same results by yogic techniques in breathing exercises, diet, sex and meditation. This gave two ways of attaining immortality suitable for different temperaments.

In preparing the elixir there are instructions as to the control of the heat, always an important point in eastern and western alchemy:

The flame at the start should be weak as to be controllable and should be made strong at the end. Close attention and careful watch should be given so as to regulate properly the heat or cold. There are twelve divisions to the cycle. On completion of the cycle a closer watch should be accorded. As the breath expires, life is ended. Death expels the spirit. The colour changes to a purple. Behold! Returned medicine *[huan tan]* is obtained. This is then made into pills. These are extremely efficacious, although their individual size is so small that they occupy only the point of a knife or the edge of a spatula.

If the compounding of the elixir is not properly carried out 'law and order will be upset' and failure is inevitable, 'for this is just as absurd as attempting to repair a cauldron with glue, or to get rid of cold with ice, or as reports of flying tortoises or dancing snakes.'

On the esoteric level this control of the heat symbolizes the need for a slow pace, within the capacities of the pupil, at the beginning of the work; it warns the alchemist not to try and run before learning to walk.

The 'Returned Medicine' or 'Reverted Elixir,' the most prized and efficacious of all, is the 'nine-times cycled elixir.' This was placed in a reaction vessel and exposed to the sun after the summer solstice. When the container became hot a pound of cinnabar was put under the lid and 'even while you are watching, with the full power of the sun shining upon it, the whole content will suddenly glow and sparkle with all the colours of divine light. It will immediately turn into reverted elixir.' After taking a spoonful of this you will unquestionably rise straight up to heaven in broad daylight.

In the refining process the highly significant number nine is constantly employed. There was the Divine Nine Turn Method: putting the cinnabar through nine different processes in order to refine it to the highest quality. It was 'nine times subjected to the fire at nine regular intervals of time.' This nine-times cleansing also appears in western alchemy. The essential method in Chinese alchemy appears to have been repeated conversion from a solid state to a vapour, by heat in a sealed vessel, then allowing solidification again, this process being cyclic or a 'turn.'

In the process of obtaining the elixir there are the stages of 'red and white,' familiar to both East and West. 'You must wash it until it becomes white and beat it until it becomes red, then you will have an elixir which will endow you with ten thousand years of longevity.' This symbolism appears universally in alchemy and is bound up with the idea of the alchemist as midwife assisting the birth of the ore from the womb of the Earth Mother. This is the white of water and the red of blood in the birth. Also the white flower is silver, the feminine; the red flower gold, the masculine; both are contained in the elixir and in the philosophers' egg and grew out of it as a symbol of creation. In the West the white rose, or lily, is the Queen, the red rose is the King. The white, as water, and the red as fire are the two great powers of creation and destruction in the world. In Arabic alchemy Senior said that in purifying the mind every black thing is made white and every white thing red, 'for water whitens and fire gives light.'

On the exoteric plane there was much in common between the elixir and the magic potions or powers of fairy tales, such as the magic table, already referred to, which appeared when summoned to provide food and drink and, in alchemy, cups of jade and plates of gold; also the power of seeing events hundreds of miles distant, being immune from all natural forces and of being served by the fairy world. There were alchemical recipes for potions or ointments which made it possible to perform all these wonders. These were also the *siddhi* powers of the yogins in all eastern religions. On both the exoteric and esoteric levels the elixir was recognized as a time-controlling substance. Ko Hung says on this: 'once one's immortality has been assured one is never again concerned about the fleeting of time.'

Sun Ssu-mo, who had made a study of alchemy, wrote: 'The formulae I have studied are by no means few. On the whole they are obscure and enigmatic. Those who dip into them become increasingly bemused, and amateurs only more addled . . . that is surely not because the ancients have spoken deceiving words. It must be that students of the Way themselves have been unable to reach the essential meanings.' For these 'essential meanings' one might quote Titus Burckhardt in saying that the elixir 'unites in itself all the powers of the soul and thus acts as a transmuting "ferment" on the psychic world, and, in an indirect fashion, on the outward world also.'

The elixir is, at any level, the passing from death to life.

6

MEDICINES

The border line between the elixir and medicines is vague and ill-defined. The elixir is frequently referred to as 'the medicine' and was also known as *hsien* drugs; both were made on the assumption that there was a possibility of finding a method of controlling ageing and decay, even death itself, and though the elixir might kill the physical body, the subtle body would survive if sufficiently rarefied. Ko Hung wrote: 'By taking these two things [the elixir and gold] man can refine his body so that he never grows old and never dies. Seeking for these external substances to fortify and strengthen oneself is like feeding a flame with oil, so that it does not die out.'

That the elixir and medicines were interchangeable is shown by the list of diseases that could be cured by an elixir, such as the Cyclically Transformed Elixir, which cures nerve palpitations, poisoning, possession by demons, heart attacks, seasonal epidemics and fevers; it also appears to act as a tranquillizer since it 'pacifies the mind;' it is good for the complexion and improves sight and hearing. Having as its ingredients quicksilver, sulphur, cinnabar, powdered rhinoceros horn and musk, it is sublimated, ground, and mixed with a paste to form pills of which varying quantities were prescribed for different ailments. There are other recipes which cure epilepsy, melancholia and aid the circulation; some can 'quiet the soul and put it in touch with the Immortals.' Another elixir could revive the dead provided they had not been dead more than three days; it could also cure blindness and deafness and even ensure that things do not get lost since, once rubbed with the elixir, they will find their own way back home.

Another nine-fold elixir was received supernaturally. This was the Ninefold Perfected Jade Elixir, which was simpler to concoct than the Nine-Cycled Elixir. It was based on the nine-stalked purple mushroom and a jade infusion of vermilion and had extraordinary powers; it could halt the flow of a stream, seal a door so that one thousand men could not tug it open, open mountains and transfix brigands. Taken as a medicine it would provide immediate death if one wished to join the Immortals forthwith, or in moderate doses it would confer physical longevity and ultimate immortality.

As drugs of immortality, the elixir and medicines mentioned are mostly unidentifiable, but those that can be recognized often contained highly toxic and dangerous ingredients, minerals and plants—such as arsenic, mercury, lead, gold, digitalis, aconite and hemp, which, taken in small doses might prove stimulating at first, have curative properties, give psychedelic experiences. As Ko Hung says: 'You can even make everyone see mountains moving and trees transporting themselves, although no actual movement takes place.' If taken in large doses these ingredients would confer immortality by translation to the next world, either as intended, or quicker than was bargained for if the properties were not understood. Symptoms of poisoning were often hailed as signs that the elixir was working and 'dispelling latent disorders.' There was also a widespread belief, not confined to the East or to alchemists, that the more unpleasant the medicine the better the effect. 'After taking the elixir, if your face and body itch as though insects were crawling over them, if your hands and feet swell with dropsy, if you cannot stand the smell of food and bring it up when you eat it, if you feel sick, if your limbs are weak, if you are prone to diarrhea or vomiting, or if you have stomach aches, do not be disturbed, these are merely proofs that the elixir is succeeding in driving out the illness.'

Nor was the use of these medicines abandoned after the death of some of the experimenters trying out their own recipes or giving them to others. There was the famous instance of this happening to the T'ang Emperor Hsuan Tsung, who, after taking a dose of the magic drug, prematurely joined his ancestors and the Immortals in the next world instead of prolonging his life in this as intended.

Sun Ssu-mo said: 'Although mineral pot-pourri can be taken orally, this is really not a practice to be continued over long periods.' He regarded taking minerals as medicines as being responsible for his suffering from carbuncles and said he had seen others suffering in the same way. He concluded that he would rather eat the poisonous gelsemium root than minerals; 'understanding their toxicity one must needs be cautious.'

Some of the medicines seem to have had unforseen and disastrous effects. One adept, Ssu-ma Chi-Chu, took Cloud Powder to mount to heaven, but his head and his feet landed in different places. Another, Mo Ti, after taking the Rainbow Elixir, jumped into the river and yet another, the Master Ning, swallowed the Eaglestone Elixir and threw himself into the fire. The Lang-kan Elixir had the effect of causing intense pain in the heart, followed by a great thirst which, when assuaged, cut off the breath.

There seems little doubt, however, that some of these lethal preparations were taken with the full knowledge of their effects and that the subsequent death was a deliberate journey to the next world, in full faith of attaining immortality. Death by taking the elixir was sometimes represented as a response to a summons from the Immortals to join them in the heavens, as in the case of the young visionary Chan Tzu-liang, a youth of exceptional powers and promise who intentionally took the fatal dose.

On the other hand, some masters seemed to have complete control over the elixir and its effects. The famous alchemist Wei Po-yang, author of the *Ts'an T'ung Ch'i*, whose biography appears in the Chinese Encyclopaedia of Bibliography,

> entered the mountain to make efficacious medicines. With him were three disciples, two of whom he thought lacking in complete faith. When the medicine was made he tested them. He said: 'The good medicine is made but it ought first to be tested on the dog. If no harm comes to the dog, we may then take it ourselves, but if the dog dies of it we ought not to take it.' (Now Po-yang had brought his white dog with him to the mountain. If the number of the treatments of the medicine had not been sufficient, or if harmonious compounding had not reached the required standard, it would contain a little poison and would cause temporary death.) Po-yang gave the medicine to the dog and the dog died an instantaneous death. Whereupon he said: 'The medicine is not yet done. The dog has died of it. Doesn't this show that the divine light has not been attained? If we take it ourselves I am afraid we shall go the same way as the dog—what is to be done? The disciples asked: 'Would you take it yourself: Sir?' To which Po yang replied: 'I have abandoned the worldly route and forsaken my home and come here. I should be ashamed to return if I could not attain the *hsien*.

Wei Po-yang, his disciple Yü-sheng and the dog.

So to live without taking the medicine would be just the same as to die of the medicine. I must take it.' With these final words he put the medicine in his mouth and died instantly. On seeing this, one of the disciples said: 'Our Teacher was no common person. He took the medicine and died of it. He must have done that with special intention.' The disciple also took the medicine and died. Then the other two said to each other: 'The purpose of making medicine is to attempt to attain longevity. Now the taking of the medicine has caused deaths. It would be better not to take the medicine and so be able to live a few decades longer.' They then left the mountain together without taking the medicine, intending to get burial supplies for their Master and fellow disciple. After the departure of the disciples Po-yang revived. He placed some well-concocted medicine in the mouth of the disciple and the mouth of the dog. In a few moments they both revived. He took the disciple, whose name was Yü, and the dog and all three went the way of the Immortals. By a wood-cutter whom they met he sent a letter of thanks for the funeral arrangements to the two disciples. The two were filled with regret when they read the letter.[1]

Another more mundane use of the elixir was that it could be used as a substitute for food, in which case it did not matter whether a person 'eats a hundred times a day, or only once in a hundred days.' But when the medicines are taken a distinction should be made between those intended to cure a malady and those taken 'to nourish one's nature,' to refine the body and achieve longevity and immortality. The first should be taken on an empty stomach, the second after food.

As an offshoot from medicines, aphrodisiac drugs were developed which were important to the male, demands on whose vitality were considerable in a society which was not only polygamistic, but in which concubines were kept in addition to a plurality of wives. Nor is the belief in such drugs a thing of the past: witness the pressure, in our times, on the rhinoceros by poachers who still make a fortune by selling the horn as a powerful aphrodisiac.

Many writers have maintained that the task of alchemy was not to make gold but medicines and this is particularly true of Chinese alchemy, though it appeared also in the West. A passage attributed to Roger Bacon says that 'alchemy is a science which teaches how to make and generate a certain medicine, called elixir, which when projected on to metals or imperfect bodies, perfects them completely at the moment of projection.'[2] In another treatise, drawing an association between the rusting and corrosion of metals and the decay of the human body, he states that 'that medicine which will remove all impurities and corrupt-ibilities from the lesser metals will also, in the opinion of the wise, take off the corruptibility of the body that human life may be prolonged for many centuries.'[3]

The Chinese alchemist, concentrating on medicines and experi-menting with minerals and plants, had more scope for his work than his western counterpart and was encouraged to follow his own intu-itions and judgement, while the western alchemist was tied to the dic-tates of the authorities and to fixed procedures and had to keep a wary eye on the strictures of the Church.

In the search for the elixir it was inevitable that the experiments undertaken by the Taoist alchemist would lead to important discov-eries concerning the properties and effects of the minerals and plants they used. As a consequence, they amassed a considerable body of medical lore, as well as laying the foundations of the sciences of chem-istry, metallurgy, astronomy, botany, herbalism, zoology and, inciden-tally, the making of perfumes. Other by-products were the acquisition of great skills in the working of metals for both decorative and prac-tical use; the spectacular use of colour in dyeing; and superb ceramic glazing techniques. The value of drinking certain medicinal waters was known as a cure for rheumatism and other ailments, pills were used to activate the kidneys, and there were powders which benefitted the circulation. The nutritional properties of the soya bean, as protein, now a popular item of diet in the West, were known from ancient times in China. Acupuncture, laughed out of court some years ago, is now seri-ously studied and practiced. One might add that gunpowder was also discovered, though it was not used for aggression or destruction but for entertainment and fireworks.

With the herbal lore of the Taoist-alchemist naturally went the practice of healing and it followed that many of the *hsien* were prac-tising doctors. Such a one was Hua T'o, of the Later Han dynasty, who was known to have discovered and used anaesthetics. He had a 'hemp-bubble-powder,' mixed with wine, which first made the patient intoxicated then unconscious. He also had a 'marvellous ointment' which caused surgical wounds to heal in four to five days. He was apparently a skilled surgeon, removing 'morbid growths and contaminating matter which caused infection.' He was reputed to have met two ancient Sages in a cave in the mountains and humbly besought them to impart their lore to him. This they did on condition that he 'took no account of the vicissitudes of fortune and was indifferent to poverty and wealth alike, high rank, or humble station, if money-making were not his aim and if his urgent desire were to bring comfort to old age and sympathy to the young.' They left him a huge volume of lore and disappeared, the cave became enveloped in swirling mists and the mountain collapsed. It was said of Huo T'o that when he was a hundred years old he had the complexion of a man in the prime of life. There is evidence that heart transplants were carried out: Ko Hung states that he had seen doctors graft on a severed finger and that trepanning took place, the cranium being opened 'to re-arrange the brain;' he said he had seen this done.

The most astounding of all, however, was the discovery in 1972 of the preservation of a corpse, for some two thousand years, by methods not known to modern science. To quote Professor Needham's account:

An unprecedented finding showed that the ancient Taoists knew how to achieve an almost perpetual conservation. A large tomb excavated by Ma-wang Tai, near Ch'angsha, proved to be that of a Lady of Tai, apparently the wife of the First Lord of that ilk . . . enfeoffed in −193. She would have died about −186 and the painted outer coffins were filled with a great variety of rich and beautiful objects, then sealed tightly with layers of charcoal and a kind of sticky white clay. So far nothing unique, but when the body was finally uncovered it was found to be like that of a person who had died only a week or two before. The elasticity of the subcutaneous tissues was conserved in an extraordinary way, for when the skin was pressed it at once returned to the normal when the pressure was released. Similarly, preservative solutions when injected raised swellings which after a short time subsided. The body was partly immersed in a brown aqueous liquid, which contained mercuric sulphide, the atmosphere in the coffin was largely methane under some pressure, the temperature had been constant at about 13°C and the coffin complex had been airtight and watertight.

Other experts suggest that the Lady might have been a consort of the Emperor Wu, who took an intense interest in alchemy. Chinese scientists, X-raying the body later, came to the conclusion that she had died of a heart attack, but also had tuberculosis, gallstones and rheumatism. Also in the tomb were some herbal medicines such as are used in cases of heart disease today.

7

MINERALS AND PLANTS

The elixir and medicines were made from either vegetable, mineral or animal elements, but mostly from the first two; there were also recipes that combined these ingredients. Herbal medicines and drugs play a more important part in Chinese alchemy than in the western branches. Plant-produced drugs were supposed to give quick but more transient results, while those from minerals were slower but surer. 'Refined pine, cypress and thistles can be taken but they are inferior to the great medicines [gold and cinnabar] and last only ten years or less,' Ko Hung maintained. It was argued that gold and jade were better ingredients than herbs since herbs decayed when buried, softened when cooked and turned to ashes when burned; if they could not maintain themselves, it was argued, how could they give lasting life to others? But although authorities like Ko Hung assert that metals produce better results in this world, it must be remembered that the Immortals on the Isle of P'eng lai used herbs, since the herbs of immortality grew there and it was to obtain these that the various expeditions were mounted.

Amongst plants, the pine and peach are the most frequently mentioned. Pine needles, roots and resin were considered highly efficacious. One lady *hsien* lived entirely on a diet of pine needles and dew. The peach, like the Tree of Life in the Western Paradise, is a fairy fruit, one bite of which automatically confers immortality. There was also the unidentified plant called *chih,* the most desirable of all; it is referred to as 'the divine herb,' the 'plant of immortality.' It grew in the Isles of the Immortals but could also be found by mortals 'in steep and dangerous places, and on high mountains and in deep valleys.'

One of the most famous pills of longevity was the Fo-ti Ting, which was said to contain kolo nuts, meadowsweet and *hydrocotya asiatica minor.* This was the medicine which the herbalist Li-chung claimed as the source of his longevity—and he should know, having lived 256 years and outlived twenty-three wives. He is an historical person and his authenticated dates were 1677-1933. He was said to look like a man in the prime of life and could outstrip young men in walking. He practised Taoist yoga and advocated 'inner quiet' as the chief means of attaining a long life.

The mushroom, the 'magic fungus', the *ling-chih*, is the most important of plants and pre-eminent for its rejuvenating qualities. It is frequently referred to, which is not surprising in view of the known psychedelic and hallucinogenic properties of some fungi. These fungi were widely used in Chinese art, together with the crane and butterfly, as symbols of longevity and immortality.

Asparagus appears to impart considerable powers; it will 'strengthen people and cause them to walk twice as fast as would thistle or knot-grass if taken for one hundred days.' These powers became positively miraculous in the case of one man, Tzu-wei, who took asparagus 'with the result that he had eighty concubines, sired a hundred and thirty sons, and walked three hundred miles a day.' Knot-grass, also called hare-bamboo, is a restorative, but it is difficult to obtain sufficient quantities of the flowers, and 'to derive great benefit from taking it requires at least ten years.' Thistle 'makes men sleek and good carriers,' but it is not as easy to take as knotgrass, though in time of famine 'it can be given to young and old in place of grain; those not knowing the difference think it is dried meat made of rice.' There were also cassia or cinnamon and a sort of root like ginger, while sesame 'prevents senility and repairs the ravages of old age.' Pine has already been mentioned for its needles, roots and resin; but the resin is of particular importance in a diet in order to 'render the body light and prevent the onset of old age.' The durability of the pine as well as its believed preservative properties made it a symbol of immortality; all evergreens have the same symbolism, giving them value as the wood for making coffins and accounting for their presence in cemeteries. In addition to this there are 'more than three hundred uses' for the pine.

There were also strange and obscure plants and animals and birds mentioned, some of which appeared to be able to change places, for example, one unidentified plant which grew on a sacred mountain by the sea, or on an island, could assume the shape of a luminous animal with head, four limbs and a tail; this, used in the right manner, would enable the consumer to live one thousand years, occasionally for ten thousand.

Nor is it merely longevity that could be conferred by these plants or creatures; they could also impart the *hsien* qualities. The sap of juniper, if spread on the soles of the feet, enables one to walk on water, or if smeared on the nose gives the ability to stay under water without drowning; it also makes the body invisible if painted on the skin, while wiping it off restores visibility. It is a universal panacea against disease, either internal or external.

Naturally, in accordance with Taoist principles of harmlessness, animals were not supposed to be used in compounding medicines, only their by-products such as dung or urine. One of the famous early physicians and researchers was T'ao Hung Ching, who had a pupil who became a *hsien* before his master. T'ao Hung Ching then enquired the reason and was told that he had been advocating and writing on experiments which used animals and so caused harm to them. He revised his work and only used herbs thereafter and became an immortal.

While herbs were used extensively, most alchemists, as has been seen, regarded metal-based drugs as more potent, on the grounds that plants were perishable while metals endured. This was particularly true of incorruptible gold, but there is some dispute as to whether any value was set on actual gold in Chinese alchemy. While gold and cinnabar are called the 'Great Medicines', it is more likely that by 'gold' is meant the golden cinnabar, or artificially made gold. The query arises from the fact that the word *chin,* used for gold, can equally be translated as simply 'metal'. Gold was a latecomer to Chinese alchemy as it was scarce in China and only found in any quantity in early times in the one district of Kiangsi. Most of it had to be imported from remote places such as Siberia, where it was exchanged for silk. The Chinese native precious substances were originally cinnabar and jade. It is probable that much of the symbolism, ritual and magic associated with gold was imported with it from its native sources. While all other metals had specific names, the term *chih* usually referred to copper or bronze, so it may be assumed that gold was of less importance; the fact that it is not mentioned in early Chinese classics or writings before the end of the fourth century BC would appear to confirm this. It was not until Han times that gold became distinguished as the 'yellow metal'. The word is used in the *I Ching* in hexagram 21, but here it is the colour yellow that is important, rather than the metal, since yellow was symbolic of the Centre, the Earth, power and dignity, implying that man should be like gold in this respect.

Nor was gold used as a general currency, although it did appear in one of the proto-feudal states. It was its value as an imperishable substance, not its intrinsic worth, which gave it its place in alchemy, the argument being that it would impart its imperishability if taken internally as a medicine or elixir, or if fashioned into plates or drinking vessels, from which it would transmit its qualities. The same applied to cinnabar and jade. Gold and jade items were buried in imperial and aristocratic tombs and the corpse was sometimes completely encased in jade mosaics held together with gold thread. Jade was placed in every orifice of the body.

Gold was esteemed principally for its colour, an attitude not confined to China since for the Egyptian alchemist the real quest was for the golden colour which embodied the 'spirit,' so that to achieve the colour was sufficient in itself. Any goldcoloured metal contained that 'spirit,' which was also perfection; hence the Egyptian gods had bodies of that colour. In fact all metals were conceived of as having spiritual power, thus the solar yellowness of sulphur sublimates the earthly and purifies it, 'washing away its sins': a religious viewpoint echoed later by the Gnostics and Christians in the conflict between the powers of good and evil in the world. Egyptian wealth depended largely on gold-mining and the making of gold was the Royal Art, the secret being imparted to only the priests and royalty; it was, as in China, a sacred matter and not a question of producing wealth. Hermoupolis, the town of Hermes, was the 'town of the holy technique,' i.e., alchemy. Gold was also used ritually in India: 'By means of gold they cleanse themselves, for gold is life immortal.' Gold was called 'mineral light.' 'For gold is light and fire is light, gold is immortality and fire is immortality.' Gold, with silver, also had a cosmological significance as the colours of the Sun and Moon.

Chinese culture did not set store on wealth as money, while the Taoist scholar in particular regarded it as an encumbrance, 'fetters and hand-cuffs' in the words of Chuang Tzu; at best it is a necessary evil. The real wealth was scholarship and the scholar was always valued above the merchant money-maker who was, in fact, looked down on and occupied an inferior social status. The scholar adopted a sublime

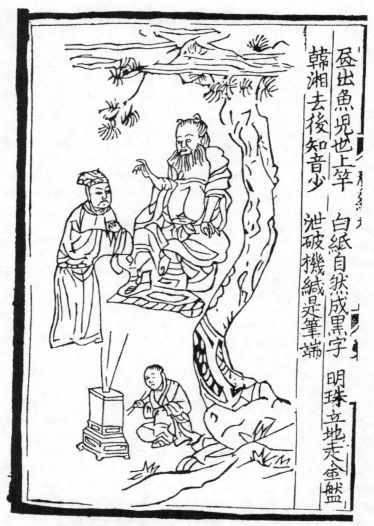

昼出魚兒世上竿
韓湘去後知音少
白紙自然成黑字
泄破機緘是筆端
明珠立地走金盤

Metallurgical Sage superintending the work.

indifference to money, so for the scholar-alchemist the use of gold was purely for an elixir or medicine. 'As to the True Man, he makes gold because he wishes by its medicinal use to become an Immortal

. . . one becomes an Immortal, the object is not to get rich,' as Ko Hung wrote. The alchemist's riches are 'contentment and learning . . . the properly balanced man is beyond profit and loss.' The Confucian school also showed contempt for material riches and adopted a highly anti-commercial attitude, regarding merchants as social parasites and calling them' reprobated persons,' subjecting them to restrictions and excluding them from official positions which were reserved for scholars. The only honourable vocations were the scholar and the farmer. The pursuit of gain was considered low and vulgar, and although officials obviously enriched themselves, such activities were not recognized and were swept under the carpet, just as the alchemical making of gold for riches took place but was not mentioned in alchemical works. The true science/art, however, was followed by intelligent men unlikely to be devoted to material wealth; to attain to the True Man was only possible for those of rare quality. So, for the scholar-alchemist the use of gold was purely as an elixir or medicine. 'When men make gold they wish to take it in order to bring divinity or *hsien*-hood upon themselves, not riches.'[1]

Gold and cinnabar, as the Great Medicines, were the most powerful and sought after of the elixirs and could be taken without the precautions necessary for the lesser medicines. However, it was better to use artificial gold. When asked why it was better to go to the trouble of making it instead of using real gold, Ko Hung replied: 'Gold created by transformation, being the very essence of a variety of ingredients is superior to natural gold.' 'The gold which is made by transmutation embodies the essences of many different chemical ingredients so that it is superior to natural gold.' Artificial gold was considered to have the added value of being obtained only in difficult conditions, needing 'seclusion in some famous mountain range, isolation from profane unbelievers and critics, religious ceremonies, purifying rites, abstention from pungent flavours and fish, to say nothing of fasting, long heating under exact conditions of temperature, needing taxing watch, and finally the indispensability of oral instructions from a genuine adept teacher.'[2] Artificial gold could be made so hard that nails could be made from it and there are various recipes and instructions as to the means of softening or hardening the metal, such as 'if too hard, heat it with lard, if too soft, with a mash of white plums.'

Silver was also sought and made artificially, but it was considered inferior to gold and jade as a medicine. 'To make silver put mercury in an iron vessel and insert three inch-square spoonsful of litharge. Fire to fusion. Pour into water and it will become silver at once,' according to Ko Hung, but he also adds that taking silver can only make you an earth *hsien*; it can be made edible in barley water or in vermilion grass wine, or in raspberry juice. Silver can also be taken when it is dissolved with large pearls from oysters; this, too, is inferior to potable gold, but the preparation of gold is not always possible since it requires the usual necessity of retirement to a mountain, fasting, avoiding certain conditions and so on: all this limits the number of those able to set about making gold. Another, and even more limiting, factor was the need for ample funds. Both eastern and western alchemists warned against attempting the work without sufficient reserves. Ko Hung emphasized this when he wrote:

> You may wish to mount to heaven by preparing gold or elixir, but you discover that the important ingredients all require so much money that you cannot afford them all. It is then necessary to go back to seek resources through farming, herding, business or trading for years and years, expending much effort. Only after that can the concocting be undertaken . . . Even then it is necessary to fast again and purify oneself: foregoing all human activities. To all these things must be added concentrated thought of the gods, preservation of unity, dispelling of evils and protecting one's own person.

Both gold and silver can be considerably debased and still look like the real metal, and various types are called 'false' and 'true.' The Greek alchemists called 'gold' all that glittered, even if it were only some veneer of gold-seeming metal, but their Chinese counterparts called this 'artful deception' (*cha*) and made their artificial gold and silver of the same substance all through. One of the side results of this exoteric alchemy in transmuting metals was the discovery of, and concern with, the making of alloys which were later used in making bronze for the superb objects in Chinese art, for both secular and religious use.

Alloys were capable of having the appearance of gold and silver without actually containing either of those metals; such alloys were bronze and brass, nickel, zinc and tin; there were also complex combinations of metals. There is evidence that zinc was used as far back as the second century BC and there are also accounts of 'yellow and white metals' which the Chinese introduced into other lands; these metals were not necessarily gold or silver but, from the records of their usage, may have been complicated alloys. Professor Needham writes of 'the remarkable fact that 2 per cent of arsenic can confer upon copper a beautiful golden colour, while 4.6 per cent makes it shine and glow like silver.' The Chinese had a 'white copper' which they exported to the West in the seventeenth century; it was used for fire grates, candlesticks and ornaments, did not tarnish and looked like silver. It was known as *pak tong* and is, in fact, now almost universally employed in modern coinage and electroplating. Professor Needham points out that the modern world owes this debt 'to the alchemical adepts and technicians of ancient and medieval China who first studied and made use of nickel.' It is also believed that the Chinese used aluminium.

Various methods and mixtures can produce endless variations in colour, from olive-green brass to brass looking like gold; copper can be anything from red-brown to silvery-white. 'Tanyang copper' looked like gold and a Chinese expression for being duped is 'to buy brass for the price of gold.' Artificial gold-making was a considerable industry and lumps of gold from alchemists' furnaces were regarded as highly valuable by foreign merchants who paid a good price for them. There were fourteen different types of gold listed in alchemy in the T'ang dynasty. The most prized was the 'purple-sheen gold.' Gold leaf was used extensively in gilding images of gods in the Taoist-Buddhist pantheon.

Although the term 'yellow and white' was used for alloys and the counterfeiting of gold and silver, it was also the esoteric name for the actual science and art of alchemy itself. Here a distinction is made between the exoteric and the esoteric, the former being a purely scientific work of transmuting base metal into finer metals, a work having no other significance than attaining health, longevity or immortality; one which Ko Hung maintained was invariably successful. The esoteric 'yellow and white' of the real alchemy was a work so secret that 'the ancients refrained from speaking openly about it and resorted to language known only to the initiates . . . much of what they say is so secret that only a small portion can be given a clear explanation.' Nor can such a work be undertaken by 'the impure and unintelligent or those with little experience of the occult arts. Certain matters can only be transmitted orally and must be learned from a teacher.' 'Also you must go to a pure spot in the mountains, so that the illiterate crowd will not know what you are undertaking.'

The most prized and potent of all minerals, though, was cinnabar, the 'red stone' or 'red sand' (*tan sha*), a light red mineral mercuric sulphide, found in Szechuan and Hunan provinces; it was esteemed above gold both as a mineral and medicine. The same plant-versus-mineral argument was used for it: 'The fact is that the least of the minor cinnabar elixir is far better than the best of things of the plant world. When submitted to the fire all plant substances are burnt to ashes, but cinnabar when calcinated produces liquid silver [quicksilver] and this, after a whole series of transformations, can revert to cinnabar again. That far exceeds what plants can do; hence such chemicals can confer longevity and immortality.'[3] The state of immortality conferred is much superior to the earth *hsien* power of silver since 'cinnabar may be transmuted into pure gold and the latter when swallowed will make one rise as a heavenly *hsien*.'

'Returned cinnabar' and the returned or 'reverted' gold were 'things of the highest importance. These two, it seems, mark the peak of the divine process leading to *hsien*-hood.' Cinnabar was purified by roasting, in the first stages to expel the mercury; after that, heating the mercury with sulphur produced a purified cinnabar or 'vermilion.' Quicksilver can be obtained from solid cinnabar by a process of roasting in a luted container; it then produces quicksilver, the 'living metal.' Ko Hung says: 'Quicksilver is originally cinnabar, which is roasted to make it quicksilver. In this case quicksilver is roasted and becomes returned cinnabar, the cinnabar returns to its original substance. That is why it is called "returned cinnabar."' In the *Pao P'u Tzu* he also deals with two kinds of elixir, the Golden Cinnabar, (*chin tan*—the Philosophers' Stone of the West) and the Gold Juice, the latter being simpler but more expensive to make. These are distinguished from the yellow and white art of transmuting base metals into gold and silver: again a purely scientific exoteric work. His recipe for making cinnabar solution is to

prepare and insert one pound of cinnabar into a green bamboo tube; add two ounces each of copper sulphate and saltpeter above and below the cinnabar; close the tube openings and seal them with hard lacquer, which must be allowed a time to dry. Place the whole in strong vinegar and bury it three feet deep in the earth. After thirty days it will have liquified and become red in colour and bitter in taste.

The red colour of the natural cinnabar and the vermilion of returned cinnabar made it of value in itself. In China, as elsewhere, red is the zenith of the colour representing the sun, fire, royalty, energy. It has always been a highly auspicious colour in China, being the brightest of all and therefore associated with, and attractive to, good spirits; evil spirits fear all light and brightness. It is also the bridal and good-luck colour, so that any red-coloured stone, and cinnabar in particular, shared this virtue. It had a particular alchemical significance in the white-to-red transformation, the powers of water and fire, opposing but complementary, in the Work. Cinnabar was *yang* to the *yin* of quicksilver; in alchemy the two were spoken of as 'the fire of the heart is red as cinnabar, the water of the kidneys is dark as lead,' and 'as medicines we value the kinds which are as red as a cock's comb and have a brilliant lustre.'

Red pigment was painted on images and sacred objects, such as buried bones, and the lettering on the bamboo tablets of the *hsien* was red in colour. This sacred-magic quality of red is not confined to China but is found in many other cultures, both primitive and advanced. It is also the sacred colour of the life-blood and this attribute was easily carried over into the notion of giving 'life' to the baser metals and to the idea of life being contained in the red cinnabar.

8

THE ALCHEMIST AS MIDWIFE

Common to both western and eastern alchemy is the concept of the alchemist as midwife. The alchemist believed that minerals, like all else in creation, were endowed with life and grew in the womb of the Earth Mother, the matrix. Metals were in embryo in the womb and grew there gradually, developing from the lower stages to the perfection of gold. The alchemist was the midwife assisting at the birth but first hastening the development in the womb and decreasing the period of gestation; an acceleration and extension of the work of Nature in generation.

The idea of the ores in embryo is also met in the term 'foetus,' used in both Chinese and Babylonian alchemy. The symbol of the Earth Mother runs right through as the *prima materia*. Mircea Eliade suggests that the sacrifices performed on alchemical occasions, occurring in different parts of the world, would be comparable to obstetric sacrifices. A further association with the embryo is the fact that the human embryo is forty weeks in the womb and the furnace under the alchemical stove must burn for the same period. African sorcerers, even today, use an aborted foetus to secure the success of the fusion of metals, 'to bring the metal to birth.'

All metals were regarded as the same in essence but in different stages of development; they could be matured and brought to perfection as gold, this being the highest aim in Nature; there was thus a total analogy with the spiritual growth of the human being. This analogy was so persistent and consistent that man and metals were spoken of in the same terms, such as the 'base' metal lead and the 'imperfect' metals as the base and unregenerate nature of humanity, both striving towards the perfection of gold, of regeneration and transmutation. Man and metals were both possessed of body, soul and spirit, the soul being individual while the spirit was universal, a kind of 'over-soul' common to all. Belief in the possibility of transmutation of base metals into gold implied that all metals are potentially gold, as the human being is potentially divine. The whole cosmos, as one living being, in its properties and potentialities, is capable of evolution and development from the state of imperfection to that of perfection; everything has innate and wonderful possibilities.

At the back of this symbolism of the Earth Mother and the reverence for Nature is the ancient and universal worship of the Great Mother, she whose body was the earth, the stones her bones and the rivers her blood: the whole a living being. It is in this original worship, not as an early science or chemistry, that many authorities see the beginnings of alchemy. The reverence for the life of the earth, the *prima materia*, and cooperation with the laws and rhythms of Nature were fundamental; experiments came later. Sciences were born from alchemy after the initial stage of the magico-religious element had declined and died, just as the great festivals, based on religious beliefs, ritual, dramas and magic, lost their 'mystery' in the mystery religions and became merely occasions for relaxation and holiday amusement. The Great Mother carries her symbolism through alchemy, in which she is dynamic as fire and heat, transforming and purifying; but in her other aspect she is destructive, consuming and devouring: both life and death.

Eliade writes of the magico-religious relationship existing between man and matter and the importance of this association in all initiatory rites, as illustrated by the 'creators', the potter, carpenter, mason, metal-worker, smith and alchemist. As he says, all held matter 'to be at once alive and sacred, and in their labours they pursue the transformation of matter, its perfection and its transmutation.' This close association with Nature and the magico-religious elements shown in Chinese alchemy are closely bound up with Taoism in both its philosophical and popular aspects.

There was always an initiatory tradition in alchemy, both eastern and western. The transmission of vital knowledge could only take place from a master to a pupil, following certain lines of working which were within a spiritual environment—that is, the sacred and the intuitive, rather than the profane and reasoning intelligence. Craftsmen formed secret and initiatory societies and guilds and, travelling from one place to another in search of materials, carried their myths and lore with them. This initiatory succession had existed from the beginning in Chinese alchemy and was implicit in the Hermetic tradition in the West.

Initiation is the archetypal pattern of transition from one state to another, from life to death to rebirth, the return to the darkness of the womb before rebirth into the light. In alchemy the 'death' of the metals, the black, *nigredo* stage, is not only the death-experience of the initiation rites; it is also psychologically the descent into the chaotic, undifferentiated realm of the unconscious, again, to return to the womb, the embryonic state from which the new person is born. To go through the initiation rites, both physical and mental, often so severe as to amount to torture, is spoken of in alchemy as the 'torture' of the metals, or of the vermilion bird, the phoenix of Chinese alchemy. For the ordeal, rigorous dedication and strength of character were required. Indian alchemy held the adept must be 'intelligent, devoted to his work, without sin and master of his passions.' Initiation is essentially a ritual confrontation with death that vouchsafes the knowledge of immortality and kills fear of death.

Two of the artificers most concerned with alchemy and necessary for its work were the miner and the smith. The miner operates in the early stages, bringing forth the ores, helping and hastening the process of birth. That he was involved in the sacred aspect of the work is shown by the fact that the opening of a new mine required a religious ceremony and elaborate ritual; fasting, prayer or meditation, incantation, ritual cleanliness and sexual abstinence were necessary as in any other branch of alchemy. To interfere with the Earth Mother is to tread on dangerous ground, indeed, in some cultures, such as the Tibetan and Amerindian, it was altogether prohibited by sacred scruples. Even on the lower folk-level, mountains, mounds and the underworld are treated with extreme caution as the homes of spirits, fairies, dwarfs, trolls and gnomes. These underground workers were always mysterious and feared for being in touch with underworld and dark powers.

'There is a vast background of myth which incorporates all transformers; among these the smith occupies an important but extraordinarily ambivalent position; he can be venerated as a god or royalty, or despised as an outcast. In some cases he is the First Ancestor who came down from heaven to found civilization. Like Prometheus, he brought the secret and use of fire to humanity and had a close association with the sky and thunder gods. These were the white smiths. Among shamanistic tribes these smiths were also descendants of a celestial smith who came to earth to teach men the use of fire and metals. The smiths' sons married the daughters of earth and all smiths are descended from them. Smiths held a high position at court, or were treated as royalty, on account of their divine descent; they were the divine artisans and the smithy was a centre of ritual and worship. Among Mongols and in Turkistan the smith was also a culture hero, 'a free horseman.' There is a tradition that Genghis Khan was a smith before he rose to become ruler of the Mongols and a world conqueror. There were also king-smiths in Africa. On the other hand, also in Africa, among the Massai, the smith was 'an unclean one' and it was dangerous to go near his hut, while to sleep with a woman of the smith class could cause a man to go mad or beget deformed offspring.

It was largely the pastoral, nomadic and hunting tribes, with the exception of the Mongols, who looked down on the smith and regarded him as an untouchable. But in all cultures the smith was held in awe and feared as a Master of Fire. He could reduce solid matter to liquid, something without form, and then could turn the pliable liquid into the solid again. Like all 'creation' craftsmen, and like the alchemist, he was a transformer and a transmuter of matter and dealt with the mysterious and magical; like the potter he turned the pliable into form; like the carpenter he brought form out of the formless, the *prima materia*. In his ambivalent position the smith could be creator or destroyer; he made both the weapons of death, the sword and the spear, and the tools of life and growth, the spade and plough. As the blacksmith he handled iron, an almost universally disliked and feared metal, though it was sacred in some cases as an apotropaic. This association with iron was also ambivalent; the metal is everywhere dreaded by the spirit world, evil spirits, witches or fairies will not go near it or cross an iron object: 'Iron scares spirits.' As an evil metal it was not allowed to be used in the construction of any sacred place; but since it repels evil spirits, the shaman loads himself and his ritual robes with iron articles and iron is used for this purpose in amulets. The blacksmith, as a master of fire, is naturally associated with the hearth and this puts him in touch with the powers of the underworld; the hearth gives access to the forces of the dark regions and the blacksmith originally learned his craft from an underworld divinity. In the Hebrew tradition the craft was brought down to earth by the fallen angel Azazel. With this connection with the powers of the underworld it was natural that smiths were credited with other magical powers, such as prophecy and healing.

Another reason for the fear of the smith was the practice of blood sacrifice, both human and animal, in the smelting of metal, although sometimes the sacrifice was voluntary. Also he was constantly surrounded by evil spirits, menacing him and against which he had to take every precaution and there had to be absolute silence accompanying his movements, all of which made him worth avoiding. Then, again, his tools, the hammer, anvil and bellows have magic powers of transformation, while the stove, cauldron and furnace all have the function of dissolution and death. Smelting is a work of fusion, the abolition of individual identity, the return to primordial chaos. The ores, regarded as male and female, *yang* and *yin,* became one in union. This has a sex symbolism which is further accentuated by the 'heat' involved; a symbolism also present in the hammer and anvil, the hammer being the formative, masculine force in nature, with the anvil as the passive feminine. The hammer is the weapon of the Thunder Gods, the Divine Smiths, with the anvil as the earth, matter. The striking of the hammer on the anvil bringing down fire from heaven, represents divine justice and power; this is why oaths were taken on the anvil, a practice which continued until recent times when marriages over the anvil, at such places as Gretna Green, perpetuated the smith's ancient religious functions.

The power of fire is also associated with the stove, oven or athanor, in which transformation took place. In Chinese alchemy the Deity of the Stove was frequently appealed to for help in bringing about a successful transmutation, especially when the recipe entailed roasting the mixture for as many as five hundred times. The stove was one of the five annual objects of sacrifice. A Controller of Recipes advised the Emperor Wu:

> You should worship the Stove and then you can make spiritual beings present themselves; when spiritual beings have presented themselves, cinnabar powder can be metamorphosized into gold; when the gold has been made, it can be used for vessels for eating and drinking and will increase the length of your life, when the length of your life has been increased, the Immortals of P'englai

in the midst of the ocean can thereupon be given audience; when they have been given audience, by making the sacrifices of *feng* and *shan* [fire and earth] you will never die.

The Kitchen God

Later the alchemical Deity of the Stove degenerated into the ubiquitous God, or Goddess, of the Kitchen, seen in all Chinese homes. This deity, though sometimes it is neither the single god or goddess but a married couple, looks after the occupants of the home. As the ancient goddess she was the 'Old Wife,' the first cook, though sometimes she is depicted as a beautiful woman dressed in red, the colour of fire; she has her hair done up in a knot on top of her head As God of the Kitchen the deity makes an annual journey to heaven to report to the Jade Emperor on the conduct of the family during the year. Both god and goddess have obvious associations with alchemy in the brewing of medicines and the roasting of ingredients.

The Stove of Chinese Alchemy is the Athanor of the West. It has many names: a kiln, sphere, vase, egg or prison, or it can be the grave, again symbolic of death and the rebirth from the womb as a place of warmth, growth and transformation. The heart can also symbolize, esoterically, the vessel in which transmutation takes place, it is the 'secret place,' and the melting of the heart is associated with the womb in the idea of return to primordial unity—that is to say, the embryonic state of the return to the origins. This, in Taoism, is the return of the Void.

There were some alchemical cults, outside the Taoist tradition, which required blood sacrifice in the concoction of medicines, rites of exorcism, or the casting of metals, but these were condemned by true Taoists. Blood sacrifice, being based on the idea of blood as the essence of life, maintained that only life can give life. There is also the universal theme in mythology and religion that the soul of one life can be transferred to another; the god dying to bring new life to the world. Stories of unsuccessful castings of such items as swords or bells, both sacred objects, tell of the deliberate sacrifice of a wife or daughter throwing herself into the molten metal, whereupon the casting immediately took place, 'life' having been given to it.

9

ASTROLOGY

From its earliest stages Chinese alchemy was associated with astrology and it is impossible to study the one without the other. Having developed under popular Taoism, astrology advanced to such a degree of importance that it became part of the government of the country in the Han dynasty and was used not only for prediction to avoid unfortunate influences, or to take advantage of fortunate times and seasons, but was also adopted by courtiers as a powerful way of restraining the Emperor from doing anything they found undesirable, since they were able to persuade him that such actions were unpropitious.

At court there was the office of Grand Astrologer, held at one time by the famous historian Ssu-ma Ch'ien and his father before him, under whom there were thirty-seven 'expectant appointees.' They were responsible for making the calendar, divining by the tortoise-shell, divining by yarrow-sticks from the *I Ching*, looking after all apotropaic matters and watching the sun and the seasons. The Court Astrologer was concerned with the state rather than with personal portents and influences. The Emperor was the Son of Heaven, its delegate on earth, and therefore under its rule, with which he must be in total conformity; to achieve this the Heavens must be consulted on all matters of state and the Emperor himself must embody the qualities of Heaven: any deviation from these rendered him unfit to rule and he could then be replaced.

The conduct of all court and state affairs was monitored by the astrologers, who read the portents and interpreted the events. Comets, eclipses of the sun and earthquakes were dire warnings that all was not well in the kingdom. Lunar eclipses, however, were regarded as being less dangerous. All this gave the astrologers immense influence at court; they were high in the official hierarchy and it has been suggested that they were sometimes, in the manner of bureaucrats, not above manipulating their astrological readings to suit their own interests at court and in the state. In the interests of security (and often of the astrologers' own!) astrological readings were kept secret, since they affected the policy of the state and foreign relationships. For example: 'When Mercury appears in company with Venus to the East, and when they are both red and shoot forth rays, then foreign kingdoms will be vanquished and the soldiers of China will be victorious.' Incidentally, as Professor Needham points out, the careful and detailed records kept by this astrological bureaucracy has been the source of much interesting and valuable information in modern times. It is also of interest to note that some of the lunar eclipses recorded were not visible at the time and place of record.

Just as Chinese alchemy differed from that of the West in searching for immortality rather than gold, so Chinese astrology differed in its emphasis on national rather than personal forecasts. Both, though, had their Court Astrologers; in fact it was said that in the West in medieval times even every great lord had his own astrologer. Early Chinese astrology was more concerned with the destiny of the state, with peace and war, the political situation and the prospect of good or bad harvests. The casting of individual horoscopes came later, probably introduced under Indian influence in the T'ang dynasty with the translation of Buddhist texts. Such horoscopes were actually discouraged at first, agreeing with the western Hermann of

The Twelve Terrestrial Branches and the Twelve Animals

Dalmatia that it was superstitious to 'account for the entire life of man by astrological reasons . . . or to . . . try to explain conceptions and nativities, character, prosperity and adversity from the courses of the stars.' But when the casting of personal horoscopes became established later it took so strong and popular a hold and became so widespread that no important move could be made without consultation and all marriages were based on the compatibility of the individual horoscopes and auspicious aspects, together with the *yin-yang* balance. If one were born at night, one's fate was *yin;* if during the day, it was *yang*.

Universally basic to both astrology and alchemy is the belief in law and order in the universe. The stars show a fixed order, clearly visible, controlling times and seasons and influencing everything in the cosmos: climatic changes, the time-keeping moon, the fertilizing sun and rain, the coming of times of storms and floods or of fair weather. In a cosmos that is one whole it is only natural that all should react on and influence everything else; so the stars must influence the formation of metals and are closely associated with them and each planet has its own metal. Both Chinese and Chaldean alchemy used astrological symbols throughout. The sun was gold; the moon, silver; Saturn, lead; Mars, iron; Venus, copper; Hermes/Mercury, tin; Jupiter, electron (an alloy of gold and silver, later replaced by tin for Jupiter and quicksilver for Mercury). As the sun was the brightest among the planets, so was gold among the metals. The gods of Olympus were also associated with these metals in alchemical thought.

The theory of the effects of conjunctions of planets is embedded in Chinese history. Ssu-ma Ch'ien notes the results of Jupiter's conjunctions: with Saturn, the Earth-planet, there is famine, political chaos and defeat in battle; with Mercury, the Water-planet, there is instability and a time of change and alteration in public affairs; with Venus, the Metal-planet, there comes a period of mourning. Jupiter (*T'ai-sui*) is also a powerful deity, the Planet of the Year; it is also the Unicorn and is auspicious for all regions and people under it and the deity can be invoked for protection. As in the West, divinities were connected with planets that exerted a profound influence over earthly matters and the fates of individuals, but in China every star had its corresponding god and metal, while every herb used in medicine had its planetary affiliations.

The planets are also linked with the *I Ching*:

The eight *kuas* [trigrams] are distributed among the planets. They never fail to operate properly. The mystical essence is exquisite but difficult to observe. It can be guessed on the basis of the heavenly sign. The heavenly signs should be observed carefully so as to ascertain their proper expressions . . . orders are to be issued according to the proper seasons . . . look above and observe the signs of the Milky Way, look down and note the lay of the land, and look in between to learn the human mind and heart.[1]

The stars held an archetypal position and the *I Ching* calls them the heavenly images of earthly forms, their movements controlling the whole of Nature.

Stars could be either baleful or beneficent according to the deities or demons with which they were associated, so their influences had to be either counteracted or encouraged. Elaborate and endless rites were employed to send off malefic stars and their demons and to invoke the aid of the auspicious star-deities. Comets were particularly sinister portents of disaster. Nor was this belief confined to China; it was almost universal and frequently referred to in literary symbolism. In the West, the Bayeux Tapestry shows a comet presaging the death of Edward the Confessor. As has been said, solar eclipses were also highly inauspicious; in fact any change in the sun foretold calamities, general misfortune or the death of an Emperor, and if an eclipse had been predicted and did not appear the Emperor was congratulated on his good fortune; an unpredicted eclipse meant certain disaster. This belief carried over into modern times; I can remember, as a child, the pandemonium that broke out when an eclipse occurred: rockets, fire-crackers, squibs soared and banged all over the place with people shouting to frighten away the mad dog that had taken a bite out of the sun. A general air of fear prevailed.

The stars, as living beings, were also portrayed as people; for instance, the Pole Star was represented by a Buddha-like figure seated on a lotus, with a wheel held in his hands to symbolize the hub of the heavens, the star remaining static while the universe revolved round it.

The Dipper, called the Bushel in China, is particularly revered as it points to and revolves round the Pole Star and acts as a celestial and seasonal clock-dial. It is said that 'when the handle of the northern Bushel points East at nightfall it is Spring through the land; when it points South it is Summer; when pointing West it is Autumn; when North it is Winter.' The Bushel is also the dwelling place of the Fates responsible for everything concerned with mankind. Like the Greek Moires and the Scandinavian Norns, these Fates also controlled the life-span of the individual. The *Ts'an T'ung Ch'i* says: 'The Bushel, being of importance in connection with the Tao, has control of things . . . the five *wei* [planets] describe their course according to the seasons. When the ordinations are not properly followed, untoward happenings occur.'

In western alchemy Fate is also associated with the stars. Boethius, in his *Consolation of Philosophy,* says that God governs the universe and though himself unmovable yet decrees a perpetual reason and order, 'sowing stars in the sky and binding the elements by numbers yet revolving the spheres and decreeing natural events in a fixed series.' Fate may be governed by spirits, angelic or demonic, through the soul or 'by the celestial motion of the stars . . . that series moves sky and stars, harmonizes the elements with one another and transforms them from one to another . . . it constrains human fortunes in an indissoluble chain of causes which, since it starts from the decree of immovable Providence, must needs itself also be immutable.'

At birth the soul enters the body through a particular star, while at death the same star guides it out of the body. Ko Hung says: 'On receiving birth and taking form in the womb we all belong to a star or celestial asterism.' During life the Bushel and the Planets influence fate, but here alchemy comes in, for although karmic forces are in operation they are not absolute since by spiritual alchemy, transformation and transmutation, it is possible so to purify and rarefy the body that spirit takes over and karmic forces are negated; in other words, the True Man is lifted out of and above the operations of the natural world.

The idea of the soul developed in a unique way in China. The soul was made up of two essences, its positive and negative aspects, the mind-nature and the body-nature, the *yang* and the *yin.* The *yin* was the *p'o* soul, heavier, earthly, which reverted to the earth at death, and the *yang* was the *hun* or lighter, heavenly soul, rising to the heavens, each returning to its natural element. Later these souls multiplied in number, there being three *hun* and seven *p'o* souls, symbolizing the

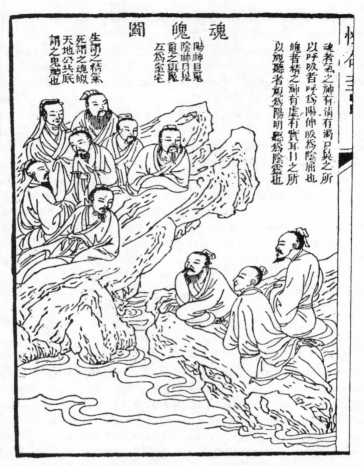

魂魄閭

陽神曰鬼
陰神曰魄
鬼之與魄
互為室宅

生即之精氣
死訴之魂魄
天地公共底
訓之鬼神也

魂者氣之神有滿有渴口與之所
以呼吸者呼為陽伸吸為陰屈也
魄者精之神有虛有實耳目之所
以視聽者視為陽明聽為陰靈也

The three *hun* souls and the seven *p'o* souls of an individual in plenary session.

different attributes of the human being. The *hun* controlled the intelligence and the *p'o* the emotions. Some of the souls can leave the body during illness and should then be brought back again. In pathological states the soul escapes from the body and a priest, shaman or magician must be employed to bring it back; it can be captured and ensnared with nets or knots and then re-bound to the body. In the case of trance, the shaman or medium deliberately dissociates the soul and sends it out to gather information from afar or from the spirit world. All souls leave the body at death, but if the body is preserved the souls could remain together, hence the prevention of the decay of the body was of great importance in attaining earthly immortality. Preservation of the body took two forms, firstly, in this life, a self-mummification was sought in rendering the body decay-resistant by a diet entailing total abstinence from meat, fish or fowl, or cereals, living on nuts, pine resin, honey and dates, and practising austerities, yoga and the elixir. Secondly, there was mummification after death, preserving the body by burying it in suits of jade, with jade in all the orifices; this preservation enabled the soul to continue living with the body on earth and, as we have seen in the case of the Lady of Tai, it was achieved with a success beyond the knowledge of modern science.

The Chinese concept of the soul differs radically from that of the West not only in its multiplicity but in that it came under the cyclic, rather than the linear, view of time and the cosmos. Maspero wrote that 'The Chinese never separated Spirit and Matter, and for them the world was a continuum passing from the Void at one end to the grossest matter at the other, hence "soul" never took up this antithetical character in relation to matter. Moreover there were too many souls for any one of them to counterbalance, as it were, the body.' In alchemy the soul is expressed as a substance to be worked on, to be transmuted, as are metals, into the noble and pure state of gold.

The *Ts'an T'ung Ch'i* says:

> Yin and yang are the regulating forces of the dwelling of *hun* and *p'o*. The *hun* of the sun is *yang* and the *p'o* of the moon is *yin*. The *hun* and *p'o* live in one another . . . the active male goes outwards, the passive female takes things in for keeping. Whenever the male goes into excesses the female is there to restore him. The *p'o* is there to control the *hun,* checking it from excesses. Not too cold, nor too warm, they go forward at the right time. They both have their needs properly met.

The two souls, although surviving bodily death, were thought to fade away ultimately unless mystical union had been attained. The *hsien* and the Sage achieved this union. As Chuang Tzu wrote: 'The

A street fortune-teller

masses value money; honest men fame; virtuous men resolution; and the Sage the soul.'

The association between the fate of the soul in this world and the stars under which it was born, and hence the importance of the horoscope in later Chinese alchemy, is seen in the story of the alchemist Cheng Wei who devoted his whole life to alchemy and obtained a servant from a magician to help him in his work. His efforts at making gold from recipes contained in an ancient treatise, 'The Great Treasure,' were always unsuccessful. His wife watched his futile attempts as he heated the retort which contained the quicksilver and offered to 'show him something,' upon which she threw some of a drug into the retort, with the result that when the drug was absorbed the contents became silver. The amazed Cheng wanted to know why she should have the secret and why she had not told him sooner, to which she replied that 'In order to get it it is necessary to have the proper fate;' that is to say, a favourable horoscope and a favourable time.

This belief in the necessity for right times and seasons was not confined to Chinese alchemy but was tied to the universal association between alchemy and astrology. Zosimus believed that experiments do not necessarily produce results in themselves but must be undertaken at the right astrological moment; the alchemist requires a knowledge of the constellations. He also said: 'It is necessary that we determine what are the opportune times . . . I have heard it said by certain ones that an operation can be carried out under any circumstances, and I hesitate to believe it.' Albertus Magnus wrote that the alchemist 'should observe the time in which the operation is performed and the proper hours for sublimations, solutions and distillations.' Geber wrote of the influence of the seven planets as the key to alchemy and maintained that the adept can find the mixture of the four elements in animals, plants and minerals by astrology. Arabic astrology says that the stars are 'in accord with all mundane creatures in all things . . . by secret institution of divinity and by natural law.' This obtained not only in alchemy proper but also in its off-shoots, in such things as talismans and magic. Roger Bacon maintained that charms and images, when made under the proper astrological influences, became endowed with power and stored the energies of the stars and the human spirit. Ko Hung wrote: 'In divining the mysterious actions of heaven and measuring the various motions of the sun, moon and five planets, we discuss their trespasses in the realms of the constellations in order to determine prosperity or decline for the future. We look upwards for signs in the skies;' 'Our kings established the office of Grand Astrologer. For appointments, establishings, worship in the ancestral temples and sacrifices to heaven and earth they always chose the right times.' And for the aspirant to *hsien*-hood: 'To enter mountains one must secure a conjunction of the best season and day, on a day and at an hour that heaven holds in its grasp;' 'Wait carefully for the advent of the proper days and hours and also observe the wax and wane of nature. A slight departure from the right path will cause immense regret;' 'Movement and rest should take place at the proper time as prescribed. Act according to the four seasons so as to suit the *ch'i* properly;' in concocting the elixir 'the sun, moon and stars must seven times complete their circuits and four seasons must nine times return.'

Astrology was linked with alchemy in the lives of the *hsien*. One Taoist, T'ao Hung Ching, had a planetarium constructed and a globe round which the heavens revolved by a mechanical device. He also made an elixir from ingredients given him by the Emperor, which both he and the Emperor took to their mutual benefit. When the Emperor wanted him to live at court, Huang Ching drew a picture of two oxen, one freely disporting itself in a meadow and the other with a golden head-stall being whipped to make it go. The Emperor got the message and laughed.

As to the Sage, Yang Hsiung was asked if the Sage could make divinations; he replied that he could and was asked then what was the difference between the Sage and the astrologer? He answered: 'The astrologer foretells what the effects of the heavenly phenomena will be on man; the Sage foretells what the effects of man's actions will be on the heavens.' Or, as Tung Chung-shu puts it: 'The actions of a man, when he reaches the highest level of goodness or evil will flow into the universal course of heaven and earth, and cause responsive reverberations in their manifestations.'

Astrology's chief message for humanity is that it is not isolated, but a part of the whole cosmos. As Raymond Harrison says, it is as well to divest the mind of the idea that it is 'a separate entity functioning apart from the rest of the cosmos' and to regard the heavenly bodies more as elemental forces lying at the roots of its own character, 'since each atom of life is the universe in miniature.'

The chief manual of Chinese astrology is the *Hung Fan*, the Grand Plan, a section of the great *Shu Ching*, the Classical History. It expands the principle of the *yin-yang* balance as active in the universe; the Sun is the Great Yang and the Moon is the Great Yin; the planets are the Lesser Yin and the fixed stars the Lesser Yang; these, in turn, are associated with the Five Elements, the purified essence of each rises upwards to the heavens to become the five planets: Mercury, water; Venus, metal; Mars, fire; Jupiter, wood; Saturn, earth, while the fixed stars contain their various essences. Methods of fate calculation were not entirely astrological since they also depended on the Five Elements principle, the Twelve Terrestrial Branches and the cyclic sixty-year periods; systems which were as much numerical-mathematical as astrological-astronomical.

10

THE FIVE ELEMENTS

In an early treatise, written about 135 BC, we read:

> Earth has its place in the centre and is the rich soil of Heaven. Earth is Heaven's thighs and arms, its virtue so prolific, so lovely to view, that it cannot be told at one time of telling. In fact Earth is what brings these Five Elements and Four Seasons all together. Metal, wood, water and fire each have their offices, yet if they did not rely on Earth in the centre, they would all collapse. In similar fashion there is a reliance of sourness, saltiness, bitterness and sweetness. Without that basic tastiness the others could not achieve 'flavour.' The sweet [the edible] is the root of the Five Elements, and its ch'i is their unifying principle, just as the existence of sweetness among the five tastes cannot but make them what they are.

This shows clearly the difference between the doctrine of the Elements in the East and West. The Earth, which is only one of the four elements in western tradition, is, in China, the central and most important on which all the others depend and from which they derive their vital energy (ch'i). The western teaching, following Aristotle and Empedocles, has four elements: earth, air, fire and water. For Aristotle, they proceed from the *prima materia,* a basic matter on which all forms can be imposed or imprinted, though itself remaining changeless. Matter and form interact to produce the four elements, which give rise to all things by simply changing the proportions of the elements, so that any one substance can be changed into another by varying the contents of the different parts, provided the right proportions are discovered. All things are, therefore, interchangeable: they are different forms of the same matter. This is the very essence of alchemical belief and work: that transmutation from one state to another is possible, that the principle of transmutation is inherent in Nature, so that the lead of base metal can be transformed into the purity of gold and the lead of the human situation transmuted into the gold of divine perfection. Or, as Marco Pallis phrases it: 'It implies the possibility of converting whatever is base and polluted into something pure and noble.' So, then, the Five Elements were not only concerned with material and seasonal changes but with the understanding of inner changes and alchemical transmutation in the individual.

There is, however, a suggestion of the fifth element in Aristotle's ether; while in the Hermetic and Rosicrucian teachings the four elements are represented by the cross, with the point of intersection, the centre, as the quintessence. A. K. Coomaraswamy draws attention to the idea of the four elements as demonstrating one of the many associations between alchemy, masonry and architecture. The four elements are symbolized by the four cornerstones, or foundation stones of a building, 'since it is upon them that the whole corporeal world, represented by the shape of the square, is constructed . . . in fact there are not only the four basic elements, but also a fifth element or the "quintessence," that is to say the ether, this latter is not on the same level as the others, for it is not simply as a base, as they are, but indeed the principle itself of the world.' Here we have the fifth element taking on much of the same importance as the Earth in Chinese symbolism, except that in the latter the Earth is also a base. In Buddhist architecture the stupa takes the form of the five elements, the square at the base

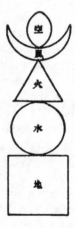

The Five Elements in Stupa form

is the Earth, the union of the other four elements, with the circle as the waters, the triangle as fire, the crescent as air and ether represented by the jewel at the top. The symbolism of the stupa form of the elements, which marked sacred places or tombs, was that the dead have been re-absorbed into their original elements.

The Five Elements of Chinese tradition, first propounded systematically by Tsou Yen, about 350 BC, were believed to be that from which all forms were derived. From this it followed that the body and its organs also proceed from those five forms, each associated with its particular element. The Five Elements and their properties are:

WOOD. East. Spring. Vitality. Production. The solid but workable. Sour. Blue or green. Controls liver and gall. The Dragon. Jupiter.

FIRE. South. Summer. Brilliance. Heat. Bitter. Red. Controls heart and small intestines. The Vermilion Bird (Phoenix). Mars.

EARTH. Centre. End of Summer. The Nourishing. Sweet. Yellow. Controls stomach and spleen. Ox or buffalo. Saturn.

METAL. West. Autumn. Destruction and decline. The solid but moulded. Acrid. White. Controls lungs and larger intestine. The White Tiger. Venus.

WATER. North. Winter. The Hidden. Cold. Fluid. Salt. Black. Controls kidneys and bladder. The Black Tortoise. Mercury.

An alternative arrangement is sometimes used in which the order is: Water, Fire, Wood, Gold or Metal, Earth. But Earth in the central position is more traditional.

The Elements also have their *yin-yang* aspects as associated with plants, metals and planets:

WOOD. Yang. The Pine—Yin. The Bamboo. Jupiter. Tin. Air. Salt.

FIRE. Yang. Burning wood—Yin. Lamp flame. Mars. Iron. Realgar.

EARTH. Yang. A Hill—Yin. A Plane or Valley. Saturn. Earth. The Retort.

METAL. Yang. A Weapon—Yin. A Kettle. Venus. Copper. Sublimate of mercury.

WATER. Yang. A Wave—Yin. A Brook. Mercury, Quicksilver. Aqua fortis. Vitriol.

These five agents, powers, or elements, also known as 'the Universal Quintet,' are, as Professor Needham says, 'five powerful forces in ever-flowing cyclical motion, and not passive motionless fundamental substances.' They are both creative and destructive; they predominate alternatively and each is followed by the one it cannot destroy; they are thus bound up with the cyclical view of Nature as the round of birth, death and rebirth, everything influencing and in relationship with everything else. This process of both giving rise to and destroying each other binds the five elements together and makes them totally interdependent, each having in itself the potentiality of the other and being united in the cosmos.

WOOD produces FIRE	METAL destroys WOOD
FIRE produces EARTH (ashes)	WOOD destroys EARTH
EARTH produces METAL	EARTH destroys WATER
METAL produces WATER	WATER destroys FIRE
WATER produces WOOD	FIRE destroys METAL

This is known as 'the cyclic conquest.' The five *yin* and five *yang* elements make up the Ten Celestial Stems (a cycle of ten characters or ideographs). Tung Chung-shu, a second-century neo-Confucianist, wrote:

The Five Elements move in a circle in proper order, each of them performing its proper functions. Therefore Wood is located in the East and characterizes the *ch'i* of Spring. Fire is located in the South and characterizes the *ch'i* of Summer. Metal is located in the West and characterizes the *ch'i* of Autumn. Water is located in the North and characterizes the *ch'i* of Winter. Earth dwells in the Centre and is called the Heavenly Nourisher . . . Water is that which soaks and descends; Fire that which blazes and ascends; Wood that which is straight and crooked; Metal that which obeys and changes; Earth that which is used for seed-time and harvest.

There is also this transforming feature in western alchemy. Alphidius says:

> The Earth becomes liquid and is transformed into Water; Water becomes liquid and is transformed into Air; Air becomes liquid and is transformed into Fire; Fire becomes liquid and is transformed into glorified Earth, and this effect is what Hermes meant when he said in his secret: "Thou shalt separate the earth from fire and the subtle from the dense."

The Emerald Tablet says that all things proceed from the One, the One divides into the elements and then recombines in unity.

In the West, too, the elements maintain the *yin-yang* quality of being contrary but complementary. Their duality exists in the hot and moist and the cold and dry. Fire is hot and dry; Air hot and moist; Water cold and fluid; Earth cold and dry.

The Five Elements are, in every respect, associated with the cyclic view of the universe, which in turn affected Chinese history also, since it was held that the dynasties rose and fell according to the dominance of the Five Powers. The dynasties also followed the Five Elements in taking the Five Colours in turn for use for official dress and occasions. (The last dynasty, the Ch'ing, was yellow.) These five colours also appeared on the pre-communist Chinese flag.

The elements played a vital role in alchemy, medicine and astrology; they were associated with the metals in alchemy; in medicine it stood to reason that they had to be taken into account since they control the bodily organs and each part of the body is affected by the others. Being connected with the planets they related to astrology, which was also closely tied to the cyclic viewpoint. Divinities of stars were also divinities of cycles, each having control of a sixty-year cycle. This 'cycle of Cathay' is calculated from the Ten Celestial Stems and the Twelve Terrestrial Branches. Each stem has a *yin* and *yang* aspect, counting as one: hence 5 X 12. Also the lowest common denominator of 10 and 12 is 60 (the year 1984 starts the next cycle, which continues until 2043). Years are *yin* or *yang* according to whether they are even or odd numbers, but cycles always start with a *yang* number and end with a *yin*. The Ten Celestial Stems with the Twelve Terrestrial Branches together form a cycle of days, months and years.

The cyclic standpoint is fundamental to all alchemy and is symbolized by the Ouroboros as the dragon in the East, the serpent in the West, swallowing its own tail; it represents the whole alchemical work. It is the cycle of disintegration and reintegration, the power that perpetually consumes and renews itself; it is also the latent power of the *prima materia*, the undifferentiated in which the end is implicit in the beginning, or 'the never-ending beginning,' or, again 'my end is my beginning.' The symbol appeared early in both eastern and western alchemy and in Chinese, Egyptian and Greek iconography. In the latter the serpent was depicted as encircling the words 'All is One.' In Chinese alchemy it is expressed thus: 'The ends and origins of things have no limit from which they began. The origin of one thing may be considered the end of another; the end of one may be considered the origin of the next.' The neo-Confucianist Chou Tun-i wrote that there always have been 'successive periods of growth and decay, of decay and growth, following each other in an endless round. There never was a decay which was not followed by a growth.' A Taoist doctrine maintains: 'There is no real creation or destruction, only densification and rarefication.'

Great importance has always been attached to the number five, known as the Magic Quintet, in all things Chinese and especially in alchemy and magic. In alchemy the significance of the number rests on its astrological associations with the five major planets (later discoveries of other planets were not allowed to alter the cosmological importance of the original five) and the five metals, lead, mercury, copper, silver and gold. These were combined in varying proportions and procedures with their five planets. The processes in alchemy were also controlled by the number five; metals should be heated, or roasted, five times, or in multiples of five, up to five hundred.

In ordinary life there were also endless groups of five: the five planets, sacred mountains, social relationships, blessings, virtues, sacrifices, colours, internal organs, tastes, poisons, tones, grains, pungent flavours, directions (North, South, West, East and Centre), spiritual and domestic animals, while five memorial poles were put on graves to represent the Five Elements at rites of the commemoration of the dead. In magical invocation, or as a talisman, the Five Elements are represented as:

I
V V V
V

Five also holds sway in alchemical yoga where the five vitalities are used in arousing the kundalini-like circular power in the body; the vitality of the heart, spleen, lungs, liver and kidneys.

Exoteric alchemy was closely associated with magic and use was made of talismans and amulets when heating the mixture for the five or multiple of five times. The chief of these amulets was the magic square, using the digits 1-9 with 5 in the central place. This square was the basis, one might call it the mandala, of the Imperial Temple of Enlightenment, used mainly for the regulation of the calendar, the Chinese years being variable in length, and for other astrological purposes.

4	9	2
3	5	7
8	1	6

The cyclic death and rebirth symbolism is also inherent in the *Pa Kua,* the Eight Trigrams denoting the eight directions, associated also with the numbers 1-9, omitting 5 since it is the centre. The Eight Trigrams were said to have been revealed to Fu-hsi, on the back of a tortoise (the tortoise-shell is universally employed in divination), and a Tibetan tablet shows the trigrams with the animals of the Zodiac, or the Twelve Terrestrial Branches, on the back of a tortoise, while another tortoise-shell appears in the centre, supporting the circle and magic square. The *kua* were associated with alchemy since its processes depended on divination of auspicious times and seasons. The *I Ching* was the basis of this divination as 'there is absolutely nothing which does not depend on the symbols of the Book of Changes.' The *I Ching* carries this cyclic significance throughout. The trigrams represent forces in Nature and the transmutations involved: 'Each in turn gives birth to the next and is overcome by the next in turn.' This is the interplay of the *yin-yang* powers and the Five Elements which are the agents or movers; this principle, carried in the trigrams and hexagrams, is implicit in all Nature.

Taoist cosmology assumes a harmonious pattern in the universe; its changes are not brought about by chance or by the arbitrary will or decrees of a creator-god, but by the spontaneous workings of the Tao: everything in it is interdependent in a cyclic recurrence, which, as Professor Needham points out, 'does not necessarily imply either the repetitive or the serially discontinuous.' He writes of the Tao as 'a field of force': 'All things oriented themselves according to it, without having been instructed to do so, and without the application of mechanical compulsion . . . the same idea springs to mind in connection with the hexagrams of the *I Ching*; *yang* and *yin,* acting as the positive and negative poles respectively of a cosmic field of force.'

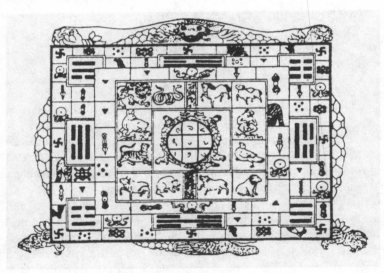

Tibetan Mystic Tablet on the back of a tortoise

In the *Shu Ching,* in the chapter on the Great Plan, it is said that the elements were produced by the powers of *yin* and *yang* and their two-fold breath, *ch'i,* which must be kept in balance to produce favourable conditions in all things.

11

CH'I

Mencius, when asked what *ch'i* was, said: 'It is difficult to express. It is *ch'i*, immensely great, immensely strong. If it be directly cultivated without handicap, then it pervades all Heaven and Earth.' In modern times Fung yu-lan says: 'The tendency in ancient times with regard to any thing or any force which was invisible and intangible was to describe it as *ch'i* . . . what is called the *ch'i* of Heaven and Earth, may be paraphrased as the basic force of the physical universe;' 'The *ch'i* is something about which we cannot say what it is . . . *ch'i* is not a "what." It is unnamable.' Ko Hung describes it as the breath or spirit by which all things are vitalized: 'There is nothing which does not require *ch'i* to remain alive.'

So the term *ch'i*, like the Tao and *wu-wei*, is not translated, being too wide in meaning for any one word. It can be used for anything of an 'invisible and intangible' nature, from gas to the vital breath of the universe. It is in this latter sense that it is used in Chinese alchemy, though in between the two extremes of usage it can be interpreted as effluvia, or any kind of emanation. Nathan Sivin writes that:

> On one level it names the air we breathe, the subtle material breath of life. In cosmology it is used for a terrestrial effluence through which the planets move. In chemistry it can refer to an aroma, to fumes, to smoke, or to the activity of a reagent. In medicine the homoeostatic force within the body is *ch'i*, so is any pathological agent which disturbs the balance, so, for that matter, is abdominal gas . . . In translating, therefore, one must choose between carrying over the larger concept of the particular sense . . . When an author specifies that the alchemical vessel be tightly luted so that the *ch'i* of the volatile ingredients may not escape, one naturally chooses 'vapours' as the equivalent which makes his intention clearest, but one loses the implication unless it is kept in mind that *ch'i* means 'activity' too.

A modern Chinese philosopher defines *ch'i* as 'the tendency to produce and reproduce, or energy.'

The word *ch'i* is one of those basic to Chinese philosophy and metaphysics and has been in use from the most ancient times. The *Tao Tê Ching* says: 'All things are backed by shade *[yin]* and faced by the light [yang] and harmonized by the immaterial Breath [ch'i],' and Hsiung Shih-li wrote: 'When *yin* and *yang* harmonize, all things are transformed. This is called the union of *ch'i.*'

The philosophers of the Han period regarded *ch'i* as the vital breath of the universe: 'the universe produced *ch'i.*' A Taoist treatise said:

> The pure *ch'i* being tenuous and loosely dispersed made the heavens, the heavy, muddy *ch'i* being coagulated and hard to move made the earth. The pure and delicate *ch'i* coming together and making a whole was an easy matter, the heavy and muddied solidification was difficult. The result was that the heavens were finished first and the earth became solid later. The combined essence of heaven-and-earth became the *yin* and the *yang* and four special forms of the *yin* and the *yang* made the Four Seasons, whilst the dispersed essence of the Four Seasons made all creatures.

The *yin* and *yang* are sometimes spoken of as the two *ch'i.*

Confucianists equally employed the term: 'Within the area of heavens and earth there is the *yin ch'i* and the *yang ch'i,* permanently imbuing men as water imbues the fish in it, that which constitutes the difference between water and *ch'i* being that one is visible and the other invisible . . . although it appears to be nothing, yet it is something. Man is permanently imbued with this stream of the two *ch'i;*' 'When the *ch'i* of the universe is condensed it becomes One; when it is divided we have *yin* and *yang;* when it is quartered we have the Four Seasons; when it is further divided we have the Five Elements. Each element has its own movement. On account of this difference in movement, we speak of the Five Powers.' The elements are spoken of as the *ch'i* of the seasons. Wood is the *ch'i* of Spring, fire that of Summer, metal of Autumn and water the *ch'i* of Winter, with Earth again as the central power, since all the other elements need the *ch'i* of earth as a basis. And it is the *ch'i* of the *yin* and *yang* that makes for the perpetual movement of rise and fall and all the opposites in creation. The concept of *ch'i,* the vital breath, like all energies and forces in the universe, has its alternating states of *yin* and *yang;* in *ch'i* the *yang* is inhaling and the *yin* exhaling; the *yang ch'i* is solar, fiery; the *yin ch'i* is lunar, watery. The *yin* is spoken of as form and the *yang* as spirit and when they are unified the Ten Thousand Things (i.e., everything in the universe) are transformed: 'This is called the union of *ch'i.'*

Ch'i can refer both to the physical breath and the act of breathing in the practices of Taoist yoga, in which the cleansing power of controlled breathing has always been recognized; but when 'embryo breathing is attained the yogin is said to be "breathing without breath," that is to say he has become one with the primordial.' *Ch'i* as breath is synonymous with life; it is the 'breath of life;' it is the breath that maintains the life of the subtle body. 'It is pure *ch'i* which charges the myriad things; where it condenses it causes life, where it disperses it causes death . . . the changes occurring in the myriad things are all due to *ch'i,* but whether they are hidden or whether they can be seen, the *ch'i* remains a unity. The Sage knows that *ch'i* itself is One and never changes.'

Ch'i is both a life energy permeating the whole being, physical, mental and spiritual, and a cosmic energy identifiable with the Hindu *prāna,* the Greek *pneuma* and the Hebrew *ruah:* it is the vital breath of the universe. 'Everything must be endowed with *ch'i* before it can have material form.' Forms are the outward and visible expression of *ch'i,* call it what you will: Spirit, breath, cosmic breath, vital energy, material force, ethereal essence; everything in creation must be in accord with it; it is the vital force, condensing and dissolving in perpetual change, alternating between *yin* and *yang* in an endless relationship, interplay and harmony, a constant flow of energy passing between them and uniting them in the cosmos. A neo-Confucianist philosopher said: 'I, along with Heaven and Earth and all things, am a cohering point of one and the same *ch'i.* Therefore I, along with Heaven and Earth and all things, am basically one body.'

A parallel with western alchemy occurs when we are told that the work must be animated by a Breath, which is the same as the Spirit which moved upon the face of the waters at the beginning of the creation of the world. In the 'condensing and dissolving' we also see the *solve et coagula,* the feminine quicksilver, *yin,* and the masculine sulphur, *yang,* being unified by salt, the unifying Spirit.

Always associated with *ch'i* is *li*, usually translated as 'principle' or 'order.' *Li* is the order which keeps the cosmos together (in Confucianism it also means propriety, ritual, ceremony and social order), the two combined comprise energy and matter; *li* is the directing principle behind *ch'i* and *ch'i* is the force through which *li* is made manifest. 'Throughout the universe there is *li* and there is *ch'i*; *li* organizing all forms from above is the root from which all things are produced; *ch'i* is the instrument comprising all forms from which all things are produced; *ch'i* is the instrument comprising all forms from below and the tools and raw material with which all things are made;' 'In the beginning, before any being existed, there was only *li*, then when it moved it generated the *yang* and when it rested it generated the *yin* . . . following a cyclical process it flows on, ever turning and returning. The Tao is the whole cosmos, the *li* the individual pattern in manifestation and the *ch'i* that through which *li* is made manifest;' When *li* is combined with *ch'i* then consciousness arises.'

As de Groot says: 'Taoism is fundamentally a religion of the cosmos . . . it concerns the universe as one large organism of powers and influences, a living machine, the core of which is the Great Ultimate Principle, or T'ai-chi.' Chinese alchemy, having its origins in Taoism, saw the operations of Nature as reflecting the divine, or spiritual, order of the universe, so the Taoist-alchemist always worked with Nature; he did not attempt to 'conquer' or subdue her. The Tao was responsible for the whole ever-changing cosmos and man; the alchemist, was the mediator, the middle-man through whom the Tao worked. It was for man to work the will of heaven. This attitude ran not only through Taoism but through all ancient Chinese thought and philosophy. Taoism never took a profane view of Nature, which was always sacred in the sense that she is the working of the Tao, the great ruling principle of the universe. Humanity and the forces of the universe interact, drawing energy from each other and pouring back that energy. Not only was there magic inherent in Nature's forces and the interaction of the macrocosm-microcosm, but, in following Nature, the alchemist, using yogic techniques, learned the perfect spontaneity of Nature, *wu-wei*. The Work had to be undertaken naturally, spontaneously, as in child's play; it was a reflection of the divine play of the universe.

Alchemy looked for an understanding of the whole of Nature; it tried to discern her secrets in a universe that embraced all forms of life, a life which was clearly evident in man, animals and plants, but which also existed in the lower forms of the seemingly inert minerals which the alchemist brought to birth. All have *ch'i*.

12

YOGA

Yoga in Taoism is essentially a spiritual alchemy. Mircea Eliade draws attention to the affinity between yoga and alchemy in that both are concerned with the soul. 'Both experiment on the soul, using the human body as a laboratory; the goal is "purification," "bringing to perfection," final transformation ... Both oppose the purely speculative path, purely metaphysical knowledge; both work on "living matter" ... both pursue deliverance from the laws of time; seek, that is, to "decondition" life, to conquer freedom and bliss; in a word "immortality."'

The yogic branch of alchemy aims, as does all Taoism, at balance. The aspirant neither renounces life in the world nor is caught up in the realm of the senses; it concentrates on the vital functions of the body with a view to the liberation of the spirit or the attainment of immortality. This goal of immortality marks a difference between Indian and Chinese yoga; the former is concerned with the control of the body as a preparation for meditation and other religious exercises for the sake of the spirit, while the Chinese cult of immortality in some cases made the achievement of immortality a goal in itself. These two schools of thought are distinguished as the masculine alchemy, *yang tan,* and the feminine, *yin tan;* the first leads to transcendence, the second to longevity. The *yang tan* is fully in accord with Indian yoga, while the *yin tan* is eminently Chinese. Indian yoga attempts to suppress the bodily powers; the Chinese to increase them to the point of total purification or etherealization.

There are both considerable similarities and differences between Indian and Chinese yoga, both arising from the soil in which they grew. There is much evidence, as Chang Chung-yuan says, to suggest that 'Chinese yoga developed independently during the early centuries of its existence, and that it had its own roots in ancient Chinese culture ... it may even have been known in the remote days of the legendary Yellow Emperor, to whom tradition attributes the introduction of these practices.' One of the differences is that Chinese yoga adopts a posture distinct from the Indian 'lotus' position; the position assumed is that of kneeling and sitting on the soles of the feet. Some see in this Chuang Tzu's 'breathing through the heels,' though others take it to be symbolic of the depth of yogic breathing. In both, the alchemical yoga is essentially the province of people who put things into practice, who 'do' things, rather than speculate on them; it is the search for perfection through knowledge rather than through faith; it is, in Indian terms, the *karma* yoga.

The highest aim of yoga is union, as the word implies; but 'yoga' embraces practices from the spiritual down to the psychic and physical in the cultivation of health and 'powers.' Yoga requires perfect discipline of body and mind, the object being to rouse the spiritual powers latent in humanity and to attain realization or immortality. Its apparent rigours are not of a destructive nature: they do not kill human instincts but discipline them into useful servants. The aims of yoga and alchemy are the same: to change unregenerate nature in humanity, that is the base metal, into gold, the perfected individual. Both speak of the soul, the soul in the body and the soul in the metals; both work for immortality; both work on bringing the dualistic conflicts of the world of the senses under control until they are resolved and brought to harmony with the rhythms of Nature. Patanjali defines yoga as 'the restrictions of the whirls of the mind' and when this is achieved 'the seer shines forth,' the 'seer' being the transcendent Self, pure awareness, a goal wholly consistent with alchemical yoga, which also adopts a 'do it yourself' attitude towards salvation. Yoga and alchemy are both a transforming of the lower to the higher, the base to the noble; both experiment on the individual; both require tenacity of purpose, arduous training and exercise and unremitting attention. It has been said that true yoga has 'a dynamic power of the soul to shed lustre;' this is the alchemical gold of the True Man.

In the unremitting attention required there are no short cuts possible and both East and West warn against by-paths. The *Ts'an T'ung Ch'i* says:

> People like trivial doings. They do not understand the long and the short of the Tao. Abandoning the right road and following vicious by-paths in the hope of pursuing a short cut, they finally find themselves at the closed end of a blind alley. This is like a blind man

who goes about without the help of a staff and a deaf man who goes to listen to music. One might as well look for rabbits and birds under water, or try to get fish in a mountain. One might as well plant wheat to reap barley, or use a pair of compasses to draw a square. Energy is thus wasted and the spirit worn away for long years without success . . . Many there have been who have devoted themselves to the cause, but very few of them have met with the good fortune of success, by searching far and wide for reputed drugs they fell into by-paths which are incompatible with the Tao. Only he who concentrates his efforts with a single-mindedness will be able to attain the Tao.

From the West the same warning is given:

I have set you on the good road; follow it always and do not take it into your head to take lanes and by-ways believing to shorten your work and to arrive sooner at the end of your desires. You would make a great mistake to do so, for it is only the great road which leads to the great work. The beginning is a little rude, rugged and difficult to take, but the further one goes, the more it smooths out and the more beautiful discoveries are made.

Nor should you 'cast your eye far ahead into a country very distant from where you are, take care not to lose your way by forcing yourself to see things to which you cannot pay adequate attention . . . the further you advance in those byways the further you will be from the great and veritable road . . . you will be altogether bewitched and not able anymore to find the true road.'

All excess must, of course, also be avoided. In Taoist yoga the Ten Excesses have their effects on various parts of the body: (1) excessive walking harms the nerves, (2) excessive standing adversely affects the bones, (3) too much sleep is bad for the blood vessels,(4) to sit too long is harmful to the blood, (5) listening to excess impairs the generative powers, (6) looking at things for too long harms the spirit, (7) talking too much affects the breath, (8) thinking too hard upsets the stomach, (9) over-indulgence in sex injures the life, (10) eating to excess damages the heart.

There are also warnings along the alchemical-yogic path that there will occur distracting or dangerous states of mind, such as visions of the horrors of the demonic world, demon apparitions or encounters; on the other hand, there may be beautiful visions, glimpses of paradise, wonderful states of ecstasy and the development of psychic or *siddhi* powers. All are to be shunned. Again, faulty techniques or indolent and intermittent practices, instead of the rigorous attention required, will lose any gains made and produce an 'evil fire' which destroys, as against the beneficent 'controlled fire' of the alchemical furnace which gives spiritual power and light. Wrong, or excessive, food and drink can also cause evil fire to burn in the body and so destroy any progress made. The evil fire also represents the very real dangers of undertaking any yogic exercise without the instructions of a competent master; this applies particularly to breathing and sex techniques. All ailments of the body must be eradicated. Yoga-medicine is preventive; illnesses must not be allowed to develop and no Sage suffers from illnesses, unless he deliberately takes on the karmic burden of someone else.

The yogin and *hsien* can always leave the body and return at will; but in the early stages of training, out-of-the-body experiences should be limited until the yogin is familiar with the necessary conditions and the practice should be limited to the day time. For six months this exercise should not be performed more than once in three days; after a year it can be undertaken daily and after two years it can be increased and may be allowed to occur at any time. This *hsien* faculty, after three years, enables the yogin to travel in spirit to distant places. In *hsien* terms, he becomes a *shen hsien,* or earthly immortal, from which, after nine years, he may rise to the state of a golden immortal, the body then being illuminated by a golden light. When, after many years, the work of transmutation is complete, the adept can leave the body and wander abroad to help heal the sick and bring salvation to suffering humanity. The principle behind all yogic and alchemical work is that nobody who has not first healed himself and put his own house in order is capable of helping anyone else.

The right posture is important in all yogic practices because it assists the flow of *ch'i;* the wrong posture hinders it. This is particularly true of breathing exercises. Breathing exercises are essential to becoming a *hsien* on the exoteric level. The method employed was known as 'womb breathing,' so called because the air should be inhaled and exhaled independently of the nose and mouth, like the foetus in the womb:

When you are beginning to learn how to control your breath, you take in the air through the nose and hold it while you count your heart beats. When you have counted one hundred and twenty, let out the air very gently through the mouth. During the process care should be taken that the passage of air either way is quite inaudible to yourself and more should go in than comes out. A good test is to place a piece of swan's-down at the aperture of the nostrils and see that it does not move when the breath is expelled.

Breathing had to be rhythmic to harmonize with the rhythms of the universe; processes of inhalation and exhalation were gradually prolonged to produce an even slower and quieter rhythm. The exercises had to be taken in 'live air.' The twenty-four hours are divided into twelve two-hour periods: the six from midnight to mid-day are 'live air' and the six from mid-day to midnight are 'dead air' periods. Any form of anger must always be avoided as it disturbs the rhythmic flow of the breath.

Breathing exercises aimed to transmute the breath into soul-substance and so make it one with the universal breath or *ch'i*. 'Womb breathing' had another association in the esoteric sense in that it helped to develop and bring to birth the embryo of the imperishable spiritual body. In the *Tao Tê Ching* the regulation of the breath is spoken of as becoming 'soft and pliant as an infant.' Ko Hung said that medicines could help in the work but breathing exercises speeded the attainment of the goal, while Chuang Tzu said: 'The pure men of old slept without dreams and woke without anxiety. They ate with discretion, breathing deep breaths; for pure men draw breath from their uttermost depth, literally "from their heels"; the vulgar only from their throats.' Chuang Tzu obviously knew of and accepted yogic practices of breathing, but, with characteristic amusement, rejected the too serious minded and vigorous efforts of the yogins and ascetics.

In Chinese yoga, as has been said, one adopted the posture of sitting on the heels (which always was, and still should be, the correct posture for women) or one might 'lie with the eyes shut and hands closed, keep the breath shut up inside to two hundred, then expel it from inside the mouth.' Ultimately one should be able to hold the breath for one thousand respirations; at this point the pulse practically stops and a state of total serenity is achieved; this is called the 'freezing spirit.' Holding the breath was also used therapeutically. The breath was 'harmonized' then swallowed and held as long as possible, while concentrating the mind on the affected organ. Here we have direct evidence of the theory of the power of thought in influencing physical conditions; the first psychosomatic remedy.

Before starting exercises 'One must withdraw to a retired chamber, shut the doors, seat oneself on a bed with a soft cover and a pillow two and a half inches high, lie down with the body in the right position, close the eyes and keep the breath shut in the diaphragm of the chest so that a hair laid on the mouth will not move.' This deep breathing, almost silent, is a characteristic of both the condition of hibernation in animals, the experience of mystical ecstasy, and of the *samhadi* or *satori* of yoga; it is achieved at both extremes of the animal-human experience; in other words, throughout nature. This hibernation-yogic breathing also transcends time and rises out of it into the eternal Now.

In Taoist-yogic breathing exercises a circular motion is set up; the 'voluntary' or ascending movement draws the breath up from the base of the spine to the top of the head, while the 'involuntary' or descending movement goes back from the lower lip, through the other 'centres,' to the tail of the spine, known as the 'gate of the tail.' This motion can set up a heat current. Each centre is known as a 'field of the elixir,' the lowest centre or field being symbolized by the cauldron. This circular movement, and the heat it involves, brings about the union of the two great powers, fire and water, the fire of the heart region and the watery element of the stomach and kidneys. It is also a reflection in the microcosm of the human body of the cycles of the macrocosm. In alchemical terms, the mercury of the heart centre is compounded with the lead of the kidney centre to produce the elixir of life. The Blue Dragon and White Tiger, Fire and Water, are unified, *yin* and *yang* are unified and the Golden Flower is born. The region of the navel is known as the 'burning cauldron' or stove, and when the vital force is roused it ascends to the 'precious cauldron' in the head and is transformed into spirit. This is the 'cavity of the spirit,' between and behind the eyes.

From this it will be seen that there is a considerable similarity between Taoist and Tantric yoga. The perfect health of the body as a vehicle for the spirit is basic to both and various techniques in Tantrism are at one with Chinese alchemy in being designed to 'destroy old age and conquer death.' Many of the famous Tantric yogins were also well-known alchemists; both traditions developed *siddhi* powers and both aimed at the same transmutation of the lower body, or base metal, into the perfect body of the True Man. An analogy can also be traced between the Taoist circular movement of the force or energy in the body and the Indian *kundalini,* the power symbolized by the serpent coiled at the base of the spine, which lies dormant until, awakened by yogic practices, it begins the ascent up the spinal region through the *chakras,* each represented by a lotus, until, increasing in power at each stage, it reaches the highest point in the head and beings about realization, enlightenment.

Kundalini, like *ch'i,* is spoken of as an 'energy,' a 'cosmic life energy;' when roused it transverses all the *chakras,* or 'fields,' upwards to final union of the opposites at the highest point. This is also spoken of as symbolizing the Sacred Marriage and in Hinduism as the union of Siva with the female goddess or *shakti.* The first *chakra* in *kundalini* symbolism can be compared with the first or 'mortal gate' in Taoist yoga, from whence the vital force ascends the spinal region; but in Chinese yoga the movement and force are cyclic, ascending in a spiral form to the 'head gate,' then returning from the 'cavity of the spirit' to the source, passing downwards again through the other centres of the heart, navel and womb, thus activating the 'foetal breath' and bringing about a union of the *yin* and *yang* powers to form a total unity in the body as a medium for the spirit. This process of ascending and descending sets up a cycle of vitality. The spine in both Indian and Chinese yoga symbolizes the world axis, while the ascent is the alchemical change from the lower to the higher, lead to gold. There is also an analogy between the lotus of the *chakras* and the Golden Flower of Taoism, in that when the yogic-alchemical process is fulfilled and the inner light is found, the lotus, or flower, begins to circulate, to move of its own volition—the Mover at Will. This is also paralleled in many western texts which state that the Philosophers' Stone has to circulate.

Chinese alchemical yoga combined both mental control and physical exercises with a diet designed to contain the 'vital forces' and to avoid any that were inimical to their development. The taking of alchemical medicines also played a part. Diet varied, but in yoga it was largely vegetarian, although the 'five pungent roots,' the garlic and onion family,' were to be avoided as aphrodisiacs, while another dietary course advocated abstaining from cereals, 'the five grains,' and eliminating fish, fowl and meat. Fasting was also recommended as beneficial and was, indeed, essential to many alchemical practices that lead towards *hsien*-hood. Eating too much coarsens the body and as the body increases so the soul decreases. It is said in the *Book of Lieh Tzu* that those who dwell in the Isles of the Immortals 'do not eat the five grains but inhale air and drink dew.' In fact when the 'vitality' is fully developed the yogin or *hsien* is said to be able to 'dispense with eating and forget about sleep,' and there were those, such as the female *hsien* Mao Nü, who, on a diet of pine needles, recommended by a Taoist hermit, became immune from hunger and cold and whose body became so etherialized that she appeared to fly.

There was also a wine which appeared to have the qualities of the elixir in conferring immortality: 'There is a jade rock on Ying Chou Island, about 10,000 feet in height, from which issues a spring resembling wine in taste. It is called Jade-wine Spring. If one drinks several pints of this wine one will immediately become intoxicated. It confers immortality on human beings.'

Many of the rules on diet and hygiene which were recommended for the yogin and alchemist are still recognized today; for example, when Huang-fu Lung met a Taoist Sage riding on a buffalo, the Sage made known to him the following rules concerning 'nourishing the spirit': 'If you desire to keep your body youthful do not work beyond the limits of your strength. Do not eat fat or rich food; use salt and spices with moderation. Abstain from worry, curtail pleasures and wrath, dismiss hurry and bustle. See that your house is well prepared to withstand the cold of Autumn and Winter and is well drained.'

All foods, like everything else in creation, have their *yin-yang* nature and must be kept in balance to maintain health. If that balance is disturbed sickness results; medicine is then a matter of finding the cause of this disturbance and restoring the balance physically or mentally by diet and medicines of the right compensating proportions.

The yogin and *hsien* used massage, and gymnastics were also practised: 'The human body requires toil and exertion, only it must not be carried to excess. It is exercise that enables the food to be properly digested, makes the blood circulate through the veins and prevents the onset of disease, just as the hinges of a door, being constantly in motion, will never get rusty.' This was said by Wu P'u, a *hsien* who was a pupil of the famous physician-surgeon Hua T'o, who himself taught the Five Animal Antics. He wrote:

> The Immortals of ancient days, while performing the inhalation process, passed their time like dormant bears, looking about like owls, twitched and stretched their limbs and joints in order to hinder the advance of old age. I have an art, called 'The Sport of Five Animals,' namely a tiger, a stag, a bear, a monkey and a bird, by which illness can be cured and which is good for the movements of the feet when they accompany the process of inhalation . . . Whenever you feel unwell, stand up and imitate the movements of one of these animals.

As for the ancient Taoist yoga of T'ai Chi Chuan, it has swept into the West and is now familiar in T'ai Chi classes everywhere. The T'ai Chi, the Great Ultimate is all-pervasive. 'Every single human has T'ai Chi and every single thing has T'ai Chi . . . for all things there is only one T'ai Chi . . . but everything in the world is endowed with it and with the whole of it.' This was said by a neo-Confucianist, Chu Hsi. As the Great or Supreme Ultimate, containing and contained in all things, it is represented by the *yin-yang* symbol representing the perfect balance of the two forces in the universe, the two powers being contained within the circle of totality, of cyclic revolution and dynamism. T'ai Chi yoga uses rhythmic movement and breath control to bring the *yin-yang* forces into harmony with themselves and the cosmos. Like all yogic practices it requires long and persistent application and cannot be properly learned in short 'courses' or weekend 'schools;' nor can it be learned from books; it requires a competent master.

The position adopted for sleep also imitates the natural postures of animals, such as the curved position of a dog or the coiling of a dragon. The correct position for sleep is to lie on one side, it does not matter which, with one arm bent under the head and the other stretching down to the stomach; one leg is straight and the other bent, the eyes should be closed and concentrated on each other. Breathing is, naturally, controlled and rhythmic and slowed down. Although Chuang

Tzu speaks of the dreamless sleep of the Sage, in yoga dreams are taken as an indication of progress until the state of perfection is reached. Bad dreams are a sign of imperfection and indicate that something is wrong; the *Tan Ching* says that the True Man is free from them.

In sleep the oblivion of death is experienced and death itself must be understood before the new being can be born. Alchemy in general, and its yogic branch in particular, either aims at death, or total transformation, which is the same thing; it seeks the death of the old life and the birth of the new. In the West this is the *solve et coagula* in which the opposites are dissolved and die before rebirth in the 'body of glory,' or of the 'diamond body' of Buddhism and the 'jade body' of Taoism. The *solve et coagula* can well be translated 'purification and integration.' Reference to the 'fixing' or death of mercury is, in Indian yoga, symbolic of the activities of the conscious mind, from which the yogin is liberated and therefore breaks through to the timeless state which is immortality. The yogin who conquers time also conquers death. As Eliade says: 'Immortality cannot be gained except by *arresting manifestation,* and hence the process of disintegration . . . one must find the primordial, motionless unity, which existed before the rupture.' The dissolution of the metals in alchemy is the death of the ego and the sensory life before being reborn as the selfless. The soul has to be dissolved and freed of its conventional closed-mind before it can become 'open' and receptive to new states, possibilities and potentialities. This is also the death and rebirth of initiation.

Taoist and Tantric yoga have much in common in the use of sexual techniques for bringing about realization, but the theory and practice of this yoga is far too complicated and technical to be understood by any uninitiated westerner. In the first place it requires a competent master; it then demands a total dedication and application only possible in a monastic setting, since times of day, of months and sexual cycles, must all be regularly and rigidly observed over long years of practice. Sex yoga deals with the generative forces (*ching*) merging with the spirit (*shen*) in the vital force (*ch'i*). It is known as the White Tiger and Green Dragon yoga, the White Tiger representing lead and the semen and the Green Dragon symbolizing cinnabar and the feminine fluid, the *yang* and the *yin;* the two are combined and fused to produce the Golden Pill, the foetus. The *yang,* male fluid is exhaustible;

the *yin,* female, is inexhaustible. This also introduces the inexhaust-ibility of love. In Tantric Buddhist legend a Sage, shocked at represen-tations of Buddha surrounded by mistresses, was told 'women are the gods, women are life, women are adornment, be ever among women in thought.' This feminine power represents the spontaneous aspect of love and ecstasy which overcomes duality and is thus the great unify-ing force; it is the archetypal feminine. If correctly used the two forces create life-force or immortality; if incorrectly used they are a sure way to early death. The generative forces must be preserved, not dissipated in ordinary sexual activity.

Based on the *yin-yang* balance and harmony, each sex, providing stimulus, draws forth and supports the power of the other. Taoism parts company with Buddhism, except in its Tantric branch, in regard-ing celibacy as unnatural and therefore productive of imbalance and neurosis. The yogic techniques are governed by times, seasons, lunar phrases and astrology; they were kept esoteric to a large extent and hidden under alchemical terms, since considerable danger accompa-nies some of the practices, as it does also with the breathing exercises. In Taoist yoga the woman adept plays an important part, both sexes being necessary to each other; but the *yin* power, as remarked, is the inexhaustible force.

It was believed that the 'reverted sperm' nourished the brain and one of the techniques was to hang upside down so that 'the essence of the sperm flows to the brain;' the generative forces were thus to be translated into vitality in the brain. Sexual techniques, according to Ko Hung, 'may be compared with water and fire, either of which can slay man or bring him to life, depending solely on his ability to deal with them.'

The marvellous powers attributed to the Taoist yogin, the *hsien,* are the same as the Eight Great Powers of the yoga of Maha-siddhi Buddhism. They are: (1) to make oneself small or invisible, (2, 3) to decrease or increase in height, (4) to have the most distant objects at the tip of one's fingers, (5) all wish-fulfilment, (6) perfect body control, (7) the ability to change anything in nature, (8) to be anywhere at will. Included in these are knowledge of the past and future, understanding the language of animals and communication with the dead. In these powers the association with Shamanism and magic is clear.

13

MAGIC

There is no land without its magic lore and beliefs in which there occur unexplained phenomena and relationships with invisible powers. These are called occult or arcane because their workings are not understood in the ordinary world of the senses and reason. In China, popular religious Taoism, as opposed to the classical philosophical branch, has always been associated with magic, stemming back definitely to the Han dynasty, and in tradition to such wonder-workers as the Yellow Emperor, some 3,000 years BC, and the *hsien* Ch'ih Fu who became completely rejuvenated after taking the elixir. The proximity of Shamanistic tribes also introduced magical and spiritualistic cults, while magical lore was again widened by contact with Indian thought, brought into China by exchange of culture when Chinese emissaries were sent to study Indian scholarship and when Buddhist missionaries arrived in China

Magic is closely associated with alchemy in experiments and experimental science, with the 'powers' of religious beliefs and with the medicinal knowledge of making potions, poisons and drugs. It concerned all aspects of life, in this world and the next, and was not limited to either. It is probably true of Chinese magic that it was, as E. A. Wallis Budge said of Egypt, 'older than belief in God.' Professor Needham states that science arises out of magic: 'In their earliest steps they are indistinguishable. Taoist philosophers, with their emphasis on Nature, were bound in due course to pass from the purely observational to the experimental . . . That the mastery of Nature by manual operations is possible was the firm belief of magicians and early scientists alike.' In fact in 'the early sixteenth century in Europe science was commonly called Natural Magic . . . even Newton has with justice been called "the last of the magicians" . . . one cannot emphasize too much that in their initial stages there is nothing to distinguish magic from science.'

Olympiodoros, an official at the early Byzantine court, in the fifth century, was a famous alchemist but was also noted for his knowledge of medicine and as a magician. He maintained that the success of alchemical experiments did not depend on the exact following of recipes but required the assistance of magic and magical powers. Various rulers and Popes in Europe were known as sorcerers: Popes Honorious III, Leo III, John XXII and Silvester II were known to be magicians, while Catherine de Medici and her son Henry III encouraged magicians and sorcerers who dealt with 'unknown drugs.' In the West, as much as the East, magicians were part of the court scene, of government and of the priesthood. Among monks were Roger Bacon and Albertus Magnus, and at the lower level among the ordinary people the village sorcerer, witch or wizard fulfilled the same functions. In China these were paralleled by the noted alchemists and magicians at the courts of the Emperors, by the Taoist priests of the local temples where the populace worshipped, and by the lower orders of *hsien* who worked the same wonders as the western sorcerer and dealt with the same practices and powers such as fortune telling, making amulets and talismans, commanding spirits and raising ghosts. Nor have these customs died out in either East or West.

Although there is obviously a close link between Shamanist and Taoist alchemical-magic practices, they functioned on different levels in that the shaman was trained only on the magico-religious plane while the Taoist-alchemist was a scholar and searcher after 'ancient wisdom' on an intellectual level, though in Taoism there was the division between the esoteric and exoteric branches, the latter being as full of magic and spiritism as was Shamanism. Shamanism, however, represents the oldest response of humanity to the world around. It is 'primitive' in both senses, in that it is the magico-religious belief of a simple and unsophisticated civilization and in being an originally pure doctrine of the macro-microcosmic relationship which has since degenerated. Shamanism still shows traces of a once highly-developed cosmology. Like the alchemist, the Shaman contacts not only demons but also cures diseases; he is a diviner, exorcist, invoker of spirits, a medium, healer, fortune-teller and rain-maker; or, in reverse, he can arrest storms; he also uses 'words of power.' The reason for concentration on and contending with demons, rather than being concerned with good spirits, is that the latter are helpful in any case and there is nothing to be feared from them; the former are continually intent on doing harm and must be guarded against incessantly. There is no doubt that the Shaman has 'powers;' even if his spirit powers are called in question, it is certain that he can carry out an ecstatic dance, in a crowded yurt, with some thirty to fifty pounds of iron discs and other objects attached to his robes, flinging himself about with closed eyes yet never touching any of the audience and able to lay his hands on any object he requires while still in trance.

There have always been two kinds of magic: the 'black,' which involves the invocation and co-operation of the demonic world and attempts to coerce and control these dark powers and force them to work in harness, and the 'white,' which deals with beneficial spirits and aims at working good and healing. There is also a misty borderland between black and white in the use of talismans, charms and words of power, practices which have endured for thousands of years and are still fully alive in the modern scientific-rationalist climate. People or teams still carry their mascots, have lucky numbers, wear amulets and 'touch wood' after any boast.

It has always been assumed that the future can be foretold and accepted that certain people have divinatory power. Oracles and seers were consulted and signs and portents read in such things as the flights of birds, the entrails of sacrificed animals, the throwing of sticks or coins, the markings on tortoise-shells; mirrors, crystal balls, bowls of water, and bones were also used in divination. Many of these practices, though, had an esoteric aspect beyond the outward-seeming superstition. Exoterically, talismans, charms and other means of avoiding or curing misfortune or calamities, both natural and spiritual, were believed actually to encapsulate the spirit concerned; esoterically, they were the means of conveying the idea of psychic balance of the forces of the cosmos and the sense of the mystical unity of all things.

In the East there was no reason why all such powers should not be beneficent provided the necessary precautions were taken, the good spirits were consulted and evil ones kept at bay; but in the West the connection between spirits and humanity was dubious, since magic had been learned from fallen angels who married the daughters of men; as the angels were 'fallen,' the arts they taught were tainted with evil.

Magic was practised not only to bring about alchemical transformations but also to summon the Immortals. The court magicians employed by the Emperor Wu were used not so much to produce gold

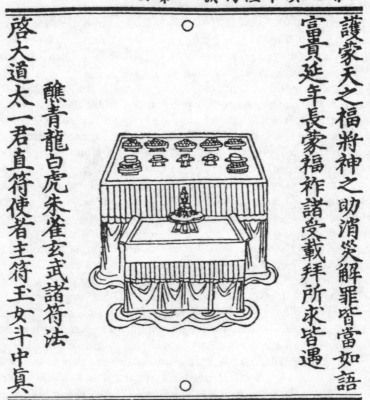

啟大道太一君直符使者主符玉女斗中真

醮青龍白虎朱雀玄武諸符法

護蒙天之福將神之助消災解罪皆當如語

富貴延年長蒙福祚諸受載拜所求皆遇

Alchemical altar with offerings

as to call up the Immortals and spirits—particularly, in this case, the spirit of the greatly-mourned favourite, the Lady Wang. The Chinese Festival of the Moon Palace rose from Taoist magic and commemorated the court magician's feat in enabling the Emperor to visit this beautiful maiden who lives in the Moon Palace.

In the realm of the occult, good and evil spirits can be used against each other, but as there is considerable danger in such an encounter the magician, shaman or alchemist must be under the protection of forces of a superior spiritual order. Hence, the alchemist puts himself under the tutelage of some deity—for example, the God of the Stove or, on a higher level the Great Spirit or the White Light. In Hinduism, the Vedas allow magic to be lawful only for the pure in heart, while, like the alchemist, sadhus and fakirs concerned with the occult must undergo severe discipline.

There are also spiritual visitants who take an interest in operations on the earth plane. As Ko Hung says: 'Spirits and gods frequently cause miraculous and strange things to occur among men. In our classics there is much evidence regarding them.' Among these interested persons must be ranked the dead who, for some reason or other, wish to make their presence felt in the mortal world. A powerful magician or *hsien* could also summon the dead to serve his purpose, as in the case of the noted *hsien* Liu Ken. He was once a court official at the capital of Ch'ang-an, in the Later Han dynasty. He abandoned court life and retired to a cave on the edge of a precipice. He also abandoned clothing and grew a covering of hair a foot long, but when visited, or in company, he could suddenly assume the conventional brocade robes of the scholar-official. He used his magical powers to help the local populace, providing food and healing illness, but a new governor of the province regarded him as a wizard and intended to have him tried and executed. Commanding Liu Ken to appear before him, the Governor challenged him to call up some spirits to his aid in his present predicament. Liu Ken wrote at the Judge's table and there followed an eerie whistling and clanking. The wall of the courthouse fell in and through the gap came a troop of soldiers escorting an enclosed carriage. The wall then closed behind them. Liu Ken then ordered the occupants to be brought out and an old man and woman appeared with hands bound and a noose round the neck. To his horror the Governor recognized his dead parents, who upbraided him for having been of no use to them in his life, since his official preferment had not taken place until after they had died; now, in death, he was causing them harassment and humiliation in persecuting a blameless *hsien*. The Governor immediately prostrated himself before Liu Ken and pleaded that his father and mother might be released. The *hsien* then ordered the chariot away; the wall opened and closed again behind it and Liu Ken vanished. But this was not the end of it for the Governor; his wife died soon after but came back from the next world to tell him that his parents were so enraged at his unfilial behaviour that they were going to kill him. A month later he and his son and daughter all died.

As a background to this story it must be realized that in China the whole family was held responsible for the misdeeds of any member and was involved in any punishment. Similarly, the entire family was aggrandized when a success was achieved or honour conferred, even when the honour was posthumously awarded; this had the advantage that, if anyone had been accused falsely or executed when innocent, he—and his family—could be exonerated and recompensed after death. The next world was regulated on the same hierarchic-bureaucratic lines as that of imperial times, when there were distinct grades of officials and classes of persons. This firm and practically applied belief in the spirit world permeated Chinese social and religious practices: the realm of spirits was taken seriously, nor have these beliefs died out, as witness a recent account of a spirit-marriage in Peking. A girl, having been killed in an accident before she was married, was saved the igno-miny of arriving unwed in the after-life. A recently-dead youth was found; the normal match-making ceremonies were undertaken by a go-between who settled the dowry with the girl's father; there was the normal wedding ceremonial and feast and then both bodies were bur-ied in the husband's tomb. The usual offerings of money, clothing, food and wine were offered at the graveside. Traditionally, all the requisites for a comfortable life in the next world—servants, clothing, money— were taken in the funeral procession in paper effigies or forms and burned at the grave to ascend in smoke to the heavens.

Spirits, if the body had been properly interred and there was a home to live in, were contented and well looked after in the ancient ancestor reverence; but if the right conditions were not followed, or if there were no home to go back to, the spirit then became a wander-ing ghost, unhappy in itself and a threat to the living; hence the many rites for preventing such ghosts from causing harm and for banishing them. This, too, explains the great importance of having sons. Daugh-ters marry into other families, but sons perpetuate the family home and provide the necessary home for the ancestors. There are various methods of keeping ghosts at bay. 'If you meet a ghost coming and shouting continually to you for food, show it a white reed and it will

Servants for the Dead Effigies following the funeral.

die instantly. In the mountains ghosts are continually creating confusion to make people lose their way.' They also cause illness and disease, but if the right magic is employed they can be controlled and made to serve the living. For this purpose spells, incantations and 'words of power' were used, both oral and written. There is a universal belief in the power of sound in words. In Egypt the cult of immortality was as much of an all-absorbing interest as in China, not only in the preservation of the physical body but also in magical formulas which helped the dead in the next world. Both Isis and Thoth/Hermes held the secret of sound and Isis revivified the dead Osiris, killed by his brother Set, with magic words; the exact pronunciation and understanding of their meaning was of the utmost importance. In Hinduism the sound OM penetrates and sustains the whole cosmos.

Summoning spirits or demons is universally done by the magic Power of the Name. Spirits serve the magicians, shamans and priests, and are often treated with contempt by the masters who exercise power over them. Incantations could force demons to leave their abodes and appear before the sorcerer at his will. Divine names were used in incantations and invocations; these were esoteric and a jealous guard was kept on them. There was a constant struggle between the shaman-magician-alchemist and the spirits he needed to serve him; either he obtained the mastery over them or they mastered him and he would become 'possessed.' In Chinese alchemy possession belonged only to the failures who, in consequence, require the rites of exorcism. Wandering ghosts and spirits could also take possession of the body of those making mistakes or trespassing on forbidden ground while insufficiently 'protected.' Possession was taken seriously and in religious Taoism priests were trained in exorcism, while magicians used their powers to expel possessing spirits.

Possession can be voluntary or involuntary. Priests and mediums could be possessed by spirits when in trance. In the lower orders these entities could be demons; in the higher states, gods, goddesses or *hsien* could speak through the medium. It was in cases where demons or ghosts took over against the intentions of the person that the individual became possessed to his or her detriment and so required exorcism. Priests, shamans and mediums, once possessed, had command over all magical powers: they could slash themselves with knives and remain unhurt, swallow fire, walk on live coals, cause objects to fly through the air or levitate themselves; such powers have been examined and attested to in modern times. I witnessed them myself at close quarters when itinerant magicians displayed their abilities in the market place with people crowding round within touching distance. Swords, offered to the crowd to test, were 'swallowed' and coals taken from a brazier were also offered for inspection then put into the mouth and held there and spat out, still blazing hot.

These magic powers were used by the 'bellows blowers' alchemists in their work, but the true *hsien* did not use the mastery of spirits in his work on the spirit; that was done by yoga, self-mastery and by co-operation with Nature to become one with her rhythms.

The Sorceress (*wu*) played a vital part in ancient Chinese magic. She purified herself with perfumed water, donned ritual robes, took a flower in her hand and mimed her journey in search of the gods or

A sword swallower

goddesses. She danced ecstatically to the music of drums, flutes and song until she fell exhausted and the deity invoked then spoke through her. Like the *hsien,* the *wu* could become invisible, levitate, travel great distances in the spirit and could produce all the magical and mediumistic phenomena. Her male counterpart was called a *hsi.*

Chinese alchemists were experts in making perfumes, which occupied an important place in all religious rites and any ritual-social occasion. Indeed, scents have always been valued and used in all aspects of Chinese life: witness the numerous scents employed in perfuming Chinese teas. Among ritual perfumes incense sticks were prominent. In Taoist temples incense burning is a central rite and traces of its ancient alchemical connections can be seen in the name of those who attend the burners or the altar—'furnace masters'. Incense also has magic qualities in that it dispels evil spirits and other undesirable entities such as wandering ghosts and prevents them from interfering in either religious or social rites or in alchemical experiments. Incense sticks are an essential part of divination, especially when consulting the *I Ching*. Other uses were as timing devices for alchemical experiments and for fumigation. Incense has always been employed in purification and as a homage to divinities; it suggests the 'subtle body' rising as a spiritual substance and a 'perfume that deifies.' It is also *ch'i* and symbolically the principle of change. The smoke rising upwards forms an *axis mundi* between the two worlds and carries messages and prayer heavenwards; it is a combination of fire and air, symbolizing the power of both, but especially the former in alchemy.

Books can also work magic. The Chinese have always had a great reverence for books and printed matter. (As a child one's amahs would never allow a book to lie on the floor or be dropped. They could not read the books or know their trivial nature, but they were printed and therefore to be revered.) Classics must be wrapped in silk and stored in a 'purified place' and 'whenever anything is done about them one must first announce it to them, as though you were serving a sovereign father.' If certain classics are kept in a house they will 'banish evil and hateful ghosts, soften the effects of epidemics, block calamities and rout misfortunes.' It also helps to give a sick person, or a woman in labour, a certain classic to hold. In building a new house or preparing a tomb, copies of the 'Earth August Text' should be taken to the site; the household will then become rich and prosperous, the grave protected from robbers and ghosts. Some scrolls enable people to change sex, age or character, to produce miraculous food, change into birds or animals, or raise wind, rain or snow.

Talismans and amulets are universally employed to ward off evil spirits. Peach stones, as the kernel of the fruit of immortality, are particularly efficacious and are frequently carved into apotropaic forms, such as a figure of a *hsien* or of a Buddha, while peach wood is used for the pen in automatic writing. Swords made of cash linked together by red thread work magic in cutting off demons and the cash sword is used in rites of exorcism. The red thread is in itself effective and red and yellow are used to bring luck and ward off evil on all occasions. Yellow and red paper is employed for charms, as being also the colours of gold and cinnabar. Bells, too, are used in magic and effectively scare off evil spirits; for this purpose they were often hung from the points of temples or pagodas.

The seal of Lao Tzu, an all-powerful talisman and bringer of good fortune, worn by mediums.

Mirror magic is widespread. Mirrors can be used for summoning gods and genii, but in this case it is important to know the names and the types of clothes worn by each, otherwise one might fail to recognize him or her on arrival and so cause considerable umbrage, with potentially disastrous results. Mirrors enable the shaman and magician to see things far off and to find things which are lost; they also reveal the true nature of the person; for example, if, when one is approached by a supernatural person, one looks into a mirror, a fox or a tiger may be reflected masquerading as a human. The 'burning mirror' could create fire and was *yang;* the 'dew mirror' collected dew at night called 'moon water' and was *yin.* Mirror magic was also used in the West to hold over herbs collected for alchemical purposes; the plants had to be picked before sunrise, under a waning moon, and the process required the person to be 'barefoot, chaste, ungirded and wear no ring.' One can also divine from sun or moon rays reflected in a mirror or water.

As can be seen from this, herbs are subject to both astrological and magical influences and gathering them demanded an exact knowledge of times and seasons; this, again, obtained in eastern and western alchemy. In the West instructions were given for finding one's guiding star, which involved the herb being gathered at the right time, in a state of purity, kept in linen, with a whole grain of wheat from a loaf of bread, then placed under the pillow. After prayers are said to the seven planets, repeated seven times, one's guiding star will be revealed in

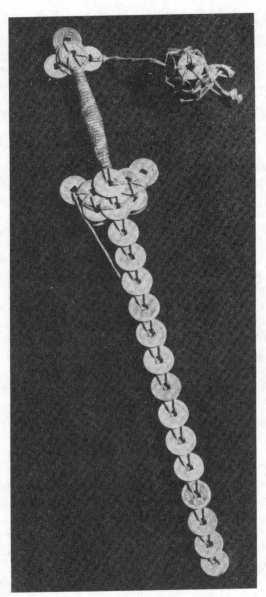

A cash sword

sleep. Magic also enters when one is instructed to make a circle round the herb, using gold, silver or ivory, the tooth of a wild boar or the horn of a bull.

Messages and instructions could be received from the spirit world and from *hsien* through automatic writing, which was known to have been used in early Sung times. It was said that the Immortal Tung Pin, after invocation, communicated through a willow stick held by a blindfolded person over a tray of sand. This method of communication is of considerable interest since it is still in use today. The willow or peach stick, or pencil, can be held by one blindfolded, or it is supported on the upturned palms of the medium's hand, a position in which no muscular control can be exerted. The pencil appears to assume a life of its own, characters are formed in the sand and interpreted either as messages or alchemical instructions. Even books could be so transmitted: the *Secret of the Golden Flower* was reputed to have been written in this way.

As in all things Chinese, absolute courtesy must be observed. A spirit summoned to give aid is offered a chair to sit on and asked to give his honourable name and to identify himself by enumerating his august titles and the period of history he honoured with his presence. The spirit is bowed to and ritually thanked for help given; in return he depreciates his efforts and thanks the company for their invitation.

There were endless schools of magicians, soothsayers, horoscopists, geomancers and those who watched the heavens for portents. There was a huge trade in talismans and charms and, on the less magical side, there also existed a science of physiognomy which studied physical features and characteristics, but also drew from them conclusions as to the fate of the individual.

Associated with both *ch'i* and magic was the practice of geomancy, known as *feng-shui*, literally wind-and-water. It was the science of favourable conditions, climatic, physical and of the spirit world and was used in locating the right situations for temples, houses, graves, or the best places for business transactions. The abodes of both the living and the dead had to be in harmony with the cosmic currents and the breath of Nature, the *ch'i* of the earth. It required the offices of diviners, known as 'professors of divination,' the geomancers, to determine favourable situations which must also be governed by the *yin-yang* features of the scene. For this the geomantic compass was used. At the centre of the instrument there is a mariners' compass, an early Chinese invention, the 'Southpointing needle', also called the *Tai Chi*. The sixteen successive circles round the compass depict, first, the *pa kua*, then the twenty-four celestial constellations and after that the various numerical and occult calculations based on the sexagenary cycle, the constellations and the Twelve Terrestrial Branches. Naturally,

Talisman of one hundred forms of the character *shou*: Longevity.

favourable sites, times and seasons also affected the times and places for alchemical experiments.

The ability to work magic is not, according to Ko Hung, a special endowment but is acquired through learning from Masters and taking elixirs. These individuals were not born with the knowledge of these things: 'It is thought that the divine process cannot be acquired through study so I would remind you of bodily metamorphoses, sword swallowing, fire eating, disappearing at will, raising clouds and vapours, snake charming, walking on knife blades without being cut.' In another passage he wrote: 'Narrow-minded and ignorant people take the profound as if it were uncouth and relegate the marvellous to the realm of fiction . . . what narrow-mindedness and ignorance.' But for all its powers he decided that magic will not be able to confer Fullness of Life on its practitioners. 'They may cure illness, raise people from the dead, go years without hunger, command ghosts and gods, disappear at will, see what is occurring a thousand miles away . . . and know misfortune and good fortune for things that have not yet occurred, but none of those things benefits their longevity or immortality.' And again: 'Only those who have Tao can truly perform these actions, and, better still, not perform them, though able to perform them.'

14

ALLIED SYMBOLISM

The symbolism of alchemy uses a language of its own which, like all symbolism, when understood, opens up hidden meanings. Symbolism is always ambivalent, on the one hand it makes more accessible and universal ideas which transcend the limitations of ordinary language and is the only language which is both international and capable of adaptation to all levels of understanding and experience and of endless expansion; on the other hand, it can be used to veil knowledge, to keep it hidden from those incapable of using it correctly. These are the exoteric and esoteric aspects. It is mainly the latter which is used in alchemy, since much of its knowledge could be dangerous, physically and spiritually, in the wrong hands. Both eastern and western technical terms were disguised under strange and often bizarre names employed for the substances, instruments and methods used; hence, much of the language and symbolism used is incomprehensible to the modern world. For example, an ancient Chinese treatise read:

> Red sand, cinnabar is of wood and will combine with metal [gold]; gold and water live together; wood and fire keep each other company. In the beginning these four were in a confused state. They came to be classified as Tigers and Dragons. The numbers for the Dragon which are odd are *yang*, and those for the Tiger are *yin* and even. The blue liver is the father, and the white lungs are the mother. The red heart is the daughter, the yellow spleen is the grandfather and the black kidneys are the son. The son is the beginning of the Five Elements . . .

As Holmyard points out, modern science uses signs and symbols, an esoteric language unintelligible to the uninitiated but differing from alchemy in that the latter's symbols are allegorical; in other words, modern science uses signs rather than symbols in the strict sense of the word. He also writes of alchemical symbolism as being of two kinds, the literary and the graphic:

Literary symbolism in its simplest form is seen as the inveterate habit of adepts of applying fanciful names to the substances and apparatus used in alchemy, principally by metaphor or real or supposed analogy. Thus an oval or a spherical vessel which could be hermetically sealed was commonly referred to as the 'philosophers' egg,' and not merely because of its shape, but with a reference to the egg out of which the universe was hatched; so that in a particular context it may be hard to decide whether the author is describing a piece of apparatus or trying to convey a fragment of doctrine.

This oval or round vessel as the egg is a universal symbol of creation. Its function is the bringing of new life; it encloses the whole universe and is the Potential; as such it is also the womb. In Chinese alchemy this is known as the luted vase; it is the place of metamorphosis from which new life emerges. The womb is also equated with the mine, the earth, the Earth Mother, the ore being in embryo in her. The alchemist is, as has been said, the midwife who brings the embryo to birth. The *T'ai I Chin Hua Tsung Chih,* a work in the Taoist Canon, says: 'The work must be directed to the warming and nourishing of the spiritual embryo.' Thus the foetus or embryo represents the spiritual development which grows until full maturity when it is born spiritually as the True Man. The womb naturally leads to the symbolism of water; the waters being the fundamental material of creation, the life substance, the 'waters of life,' the *prima materia,* the great *yin* power. Its *yang* opposite is, of course, fire; together they are the two great principles, the passive and the active; they represent all the contraries in the elemental world; both are creators and destroyers. As Burckhardt says, it is through the union of these opposites that 'the soul becomes "fluid fire" or "fiery water", and at the same time also acquires the positive qualities of the other elements, so that its water becomes "stable" and its fire "non-burning."' The alchemical fire does not burn and destroy but vivifies; it is a divine power. Fire can stabilize and harden, as in the potter's kiln, or make fluid in smelting, but it must be contained and controlled since any excess becomes destructive. The sixty-third hexagram of the *I Ching* combines the trigrams for fire and water and symbolizes the cauldron of water heated over the fire; hence alchemical fusion. The Taoist Canon says: 'The essence of *yang* is fire; that of *yin* water. When *yin* and *yang* control each other, water and fire are mutually upholding.'

In this connection mercury, or quicksilver, is particularly significant as it contains both the elements of fire and water, being liquid yet luminous. It can be represented as a metal, but because of its 'volatile' nature it is also regarded as spirit. Its dual nature makes it symbolic of the tensions of the complementary opposites, expressed by such symbols as the 'contending dragons' and the caduceus, containing and uniting the opposites. It represents the first and the last as the *prima materia* which divides into the opposites of all dualism, to be reunited in the *conjunctio* and to emerge in the final unity of the spirit. Exoterically, it is the quicksilver of the laboratory alchemist; esoterically, it is the spirit concealed in base matter. Mercury, regarded as a spirit, is volatile and transforming; it 'whitens all metals and attracts their souls . . . having in itself the principle of all liquidity, when it has undergone decomposition, it changes colours everywhere,' as Synesius said in commenting on the Physics and Mysteries of the pseudo-Democritus. This dissolving power of quicksilver is the feminine in its terrible aspect, its sign is dominated by the feminine lunar symbol as the Earth Mother, the womb of all metals, but it is also the triad in unity ☿ incorporating the cross, circle and crescent symbols; again, it is 'burning water' and 'non-burning fire,' the androgynous.

The alchemist succeeded in joining the two great powers of fire and water; sulphur, the hot and dry, the spirit of fire, was the colour of gold, but gold could be fused and reduced to liquid and so also had the spirit of water, the moist and the cold; the contraries were thus made one in gold. But the fire must be controlled and this introduces the symbolism of the bellows by which the fire was regulated. Fire must not be allowed to burn too fiercely at first; it must be kept steady and quiet in the early stages of the work; nor may it be allowed to die down, this being symbolic of indolent or intermittent effort, and of destruction. Once the fire is fully controlled the 'quick fire' can be brought into play that ignites the bright inner fire of illumination. It is easy to see that the bellows are a natural symbol for the controlled breathing exercises of alchemical yoga. The Patriarch Lu Tzu said: 'Only those who know what fire, cauldron and bellows really mean can use them effectively.'

Flight, which plays a minor role in western alchemy, assumes a major one in the East where powers of flight appear in all yogic traditions: the Rishis of India, the Arhats of Buddhism and the Immortals of Taoism, all manifest the power. The feather is the natural symbol of flight and typically shamanistic. In early Chinese alchemy the *hsien* was 'the feathered scholar,' or 'the feathered and transformed,' and was depicted in iconography as having feathers. In Indian alchemy those who have attained yogic powers 'can fly like fowls in the air' or 'pass instantaneously from one place to another.' In the West the soul is sometimes depicted as winged or flying heavenwards.

The Shaman, who adopts the feathered robe to fly to the spirit world, can also visit the underworld; but although there appear to be close affinities between shamanism and the magical element in Taoist alchemy, there is more of ascent than descent in the latter. The Shaman merely visits the other worlds then returns to the body; the alchemist, the feathered *hsien,* represents a totally spiritualized body, total freedom from the limits of the earthly and physical state, freedom from the world of senses. Flight is also often another term for ecstasy, for the mystic's experience of total liberation and freedom; it is also symbolic of the unrestricted powers of the mind. As the *Rig Veda* says: 'He who knows has wings.' For Chinese alchemy it is one of the chief powers of the *hsien* and is associated closely with the cult of immortality since it implies the ability to transcend all mortal limitations and to pass from one world to another and enter the realm of spirits.

There is the story of King Chao (515-488 BC) who said to his minister: 'The writings of the Chen dynasty state that Chung-li was actually sent as an envoy to the inaccessible parts of heaven and earth; how was such a thing possible? Tell me whether there is any possibility for people to ascend to heaven?' The minister explained that the true meaning of this tradition was spiritual; those who were upright and could concentrate were able 'to rise to the higher spheres and to descend to the lower, and distinguish there the things which it would be proper to do.'

Flight is one of the most fundamental longings of humanity and runs through all myth, religions ('taken up into the seventh heaven'), legends and fairy tales and dominates the dream world. Jung's extensive studies in alchemy rose from the discovery of alchemical symbolism frequently occurring in the dreams of patients who knew nothing of alchemy. This dream-flight alchemical symbolism conformed to the 'work' of alchemy in helping to bring about the process of integration in the individual; these symbols 'are part and parcel of the self, bringing with them something of the unconscious which finds expression in a feeling of eternity and immortality.'

There was no question of 'possession' in the flight of the Taoist *hsien* who 'went up to heaven' since the ability to fly was the result of long years of yogic practices and of the search for the elixir; it presupposed self-mastery, a perfect incorporation into the cosmic rhythms and a balanced, healthy, scholarly mind which had nothing to do with shamanistic-mediumistic possession. On the other hand, many of the accounts of going up to heaven may be symbolic of out-of-the-body experiences, when, relieved of the weight of the body, the soul is freed from the laws of gravity, or of the mystic experience of total liberation from all earthly limitations.

Although actual flight is less employed symbolically in western alchemy, the symbol of ascent is introduced in the form of the ladder. Initiation ceremonies are depicted by the alchemist climbing a seven-runged ladder, blindfolded, but the blindfold is removed at the seventh rung and the initiate then faces a closed door. Symbols of ascent all imply the passage from one realm to a higher and the same seven stages are found in the Shaman's seven-notched pole of ascent to the heavens, the number seven representing completeness as the sum of the earth number four and the heavenly number three—hence the macrocosm. The seven heavens symbolism appears almost universally in ascent to the heavens, which, like flight, implies aspirations towards the divine, reaching the dwelling place of supreme powers and achieving immortality therein. Among the 'feathered tribe' in China, the crane is one of the best known symbols of longevity; it is 'the Patriarch of the Feathered Tribe' and an intermediary between heaven and earth.

The Phoenix is universal in alchemy and is the archetypal death-and-rebirth symbol. In the West, Wolfram von Eschenbach wrote: 'The phoenix burns to ashes, but the ashes give him life again. Thus does the phoenix molt and change its plumage, which afterwards is shining and lovely as before.' It is the consummation of the Great Work, final regeneration. In China it is one of the Four Spiritually Endowed, or Sacred, Creatures: the Tortoise, Ky-lin, Dragon and

Phoenix, the last three being fabulous and composite creatures that combine both the *yin* and *yang* powers. The phoenix or *feng-huang*, is the Vermilion, or Fire, Bird, the substance of flame. As fire it is *yang*, solar, but it dies and remains dead for three days, the dark of the moon, and so has lunar qualities. Its composition is also *yin-yang* as it has the head of a cock, its eyes are the sun, its beak is the crescent moon and it has the back of a swallow with its wings as the wind; its tail represents trees and flowers and its feet are the earth. It also conforms to the Five symbolism, combining the five colours which represent the five cardinal virtues. This combined *yin-yang*, lunar-solar quality emphasizes the interdependence of the two powers in alchemy and their final union. Esoterically, the death of the phoenix, which is a self-immolation, is the death of form in the old nature to rise as the new transformed, a higher state of consciousness.

The mirror is not only used in magic but in speculative alchemy it is of the highest importance, the word *speculatio* meaning to mirror or reflect. This is the reflection of cosmological truths in the rhythms of Nature, expressed in Arabic alchemy by Ibn Arabi as: 'The world of nature consists of many forms which are reflected in a single mirror—nay, rather, it is a single form reflected in many mirrors.' This, again, is the 'as above so below' of the hermetic tradition in which the mirror symbolizes the intellect, the reflection of the cosmos. Its power, as the Emerald Tablet says, 'Rises from earth to heaven and comes down again from heaven to earth, and thus acquires the power of the realities above and the realities below.' It also reflects the state of the soul; in perfection it is perfectly clear and unclouded.

A mirror hanging face-downwards in a temple establishes an axis of light by which the soul can ascend heavenwards, but as reflected light it also represents the manifest world of illusion. In this way the mirror also combines the two great powers; it is the reflected light of the moon, known as the 'golden mirror,' and at the same time the disc of the sun. The flash of light given off by a mirror also symbolizes sudden spiritual realization or enlightenment. Mirror symbolism is used frequently in Taoism, neo-Confucianism and Buddhism, with the difference that 'with Buddhism external reality is to be transcended, whereas with Chuang Tzu and the neo-Confucianists, external reality is to be responded to naturally and faithfully, like a mirror objectively reflecting all.' As Chuang Tzu said: 'The mind of the Sage, being in repose, becomes the mirror of the universe.'

Symbolism and alchemy cannot be separated. Eliade writes: 'To symbolic thinking the world is not only "alive" but also "open": an object is never simply itself (as is the case with modern consciousness), it is also a sign of, or a repository for, something else.' The whole of the alchemical work was symbolic, covering, as it did, the metaphysical and religious aspects in transforming base man into the gold of perfection.

15

THE ESOTERIC AND EXOTERIC

Early alchemists, whose writings were purely personal and never intended for publication, could write as they pleased without fear of giving secrets away to the uninitiated, the merely curious or the grasping, but later, with the invention of paper and printing, the possibility of a wide distribution of knowledge occurred, and with it the need to keep dangerous knowledge secret and out of the hands of the ignorant or evil-minded. Thus there arose the division between the esoteric, or secret, and the exoteric or general knowledge, the one for initiates only, the other open to all. Once written material became generally available, esoteric lore ceased to be written down and was transmitted orally and only to chosen disciples who could be trusted with knowledge that was potentially dangerous or beyond the limited understanding of the ordinary individual. Added to this there were practices, formulas and knowledge which were the result of the experience of those who had made themselves adepts and acquired lore which they deemed could only be passed on to those of sufficient mental, moral and spiritual calibre. Books, then, when they became readily available and in general use, were only for beginners and the uninitiated. A book can be taken up or put down at will, read carefully or skimmed through and no discipline is involved; but esoteric knowledge, imparted by a master, demanded, first, the judgement of the master that the pupil was of the right quality and then serious discipline and dedication on the part of the pupil; these conditions being met, knowledge could be passed on by personal instruction only.

Alchemy is essentially an initiatory science or art and esotericism runs through all initiatory traditions; religions, the mysteries, tribal lore, shamans, magicians, secret societies, all employ a hidden language and symbolism. Though the secrets were reserved for a privileged elite, it was not an elite of chance; it was a matter of quality of understanding and being in the individual, and a matter of choice in the desire for an understanding and degree of knowledge which is absent in the vast majority of people who remain satisfied with the outward and exoteric and are not willing to undergo serious discipline to develop the necessary mental and moral qualities. The need for greater and more significant knowledge must be felt and recognized; nor is it enough merely to desire such knowledge without having the ability to understand it, and, in the first place, accept it as a valid system.

There were, however, other reasons for esotericism. During those periods when alchemy was illegal and could only be practised by imperial permission, alchemy had to go underground and treatises were written in allegorical terms; for example, Liu An disguised the transmutation processes in the following passage, totally unintelligible to the uninitiated:

> When the effluvia [ch'i] from the coastal regions [East] ascend to the azure heavens, the azure heavens in 800 years give birth to azurite, azurite in 800 years gives birth to azure quicksilver, azure quicksilver in 800 years gives birth to azure metal [lead] and azure metal in 1000 years gives birth to the Azure Dragon. Ch'i from the bull-lands [South] ascends to the red heavens in 700 years and gives birth to cinnabar and in 700 years to red copper and in 1000 years to the Red Dragon. Ch'i from the weak lands [West] ascends to the white heavens in 900 years and gives birth to white arsenic, white arsenic gives birth to white quicksilver and quicksilver gives birth to silver and in 1000 years to the White Dragon. Ch'i from the cow lands [North] ascends to the dark heavens in 600 years and gives birth to black whetstones which give birth to black quicksilver, which in 600 years gives birth to black metal [iron] and in 1000 years to the Black Dragon. These various Dragons give birth to springs of their own colour and region, the particles of which, ascending to heaven, become clouds of yin and yang then beat on one another, producing peals of thunder and fly out as lightning and come down as rain and running water into various seas—Azure, Red, White and Black.

Another justification for keeping the Work secret was the universal human weakness of greed and envy, which operated particularly in respect of two alchemical end-products, gold and power, coveted equally by rulers and the general mob. In both East and West alchemy was practised or patronized by people hoping for either riches, power or immortality. Such a patronage could have disastrous results for those failing to deliver the goods, so that it is not surprising that alchemists of every land and age spoke with one voice of the need for keeping quiet and warned against getting involved with princes and potentates. Albertus Magnus wrote in his *de Alchemica:*

> You ought to beware before all else of involving yourself with princes and potentates in any operations because of two evils, for if you have involved yourself, they inquire after you from time to time and say, 'Master, how do you succeed? When shall we see something good?' and not being able to wait for the end of the work, they say that it is nothing, and then you will have the greatest annoyance. And if you have not obtained a good result, you acquire everlasting indignation from it. If however you have obtained a good result, they think to detain you for ever and will not allow you to go away, and so you will be ensnared by the words of your own mouth and entangled by your own speeches.

It is not surprising, then, that all traditions are unanimous in giving this warning from the time of the Yellow Emperor, three centuries BC, to modern times. Tradition says that the Yellow Emperor transmitted the divine process of making the elixir with the admonition that: 'This is a highly essential divine process and must be transmitted only to those of the highest calibre. Although an improper person offers jewels piled up mountain-high, you are not to divulge it.' Ko Hung says:

> Taoists prize and keep secret the recipes leading to *hsien*-hood. They take pains selecting the very best pupils, and only after a long time do they give them the all-important oral instructions . . . These treatises will bring unlimited fecility and longevity to the gentle-man of perfect sincerity who obtains and treasures them. He who reveals them lightly to others will bring calamities upon all his rela-tions, close and distant. Nor are they to be spoken of maliciously, obscuring their *tao*. Take care not to copy them to show to the vul-gar. Take the measure of a man's virtue first; only when you have clear indication of it may you teach these treatise to him.

The *Ts'an T'ung Ch'i* says that the works are not intended to be understood by the uninitiated or to make sense of them:

They are so cautiously worded that they are not easily understood
by people of the world . . . There are directions for processes, the
more important principles of which shall be set forth, but the details
shall not be divulged . . . One's projects are only to be divulged on
personal interview . . . The way is long and obscurely mystical . . .
careful reflection is in order, but no discussion with others should
take place. The secret should be carefully guarded and no writing
should be done for its conveyance.

In the West the hermetic tradition, derived from Egypt, was developed in the philosophical Hermes of the Greeks, in the works of Plato
and Aristotle and later in the religious philosophy of the neo-Platonists.
This passed into medieval Christianity, which fused with the Arabic,
Syrian and Hebrew elements, all influenced by Babylonian and Chaldean lore. All carry the same instructions. Aristotle says in his *liber
Secretorum*: 'He is a breaker of the heavenly seal who communicates
the secrets of Nature and of Art . . . many evils follow the man who
reveals secrets.' Albertus Magnus in his tract *de Alchemica* writes:
'Wherefore I abjure you, by the Creator of the World, that you hide
this book from all stupid persons. To you indeed I will reveal the
Secret, but from others I conceal the Secret of Secrets because of the
envy of the noble science. For the stupid despise it because they are
unable to grasp it, and thence hold it hateful and believe it not to be
possible, and so envy those who work it and call them forgers. Therefore beware lest you reveal any of our secrets in this operation.' Roger
Bacon says, laconically: 'Keep this secret most secret,' while Alphidius
wrote that 'the philosophers who have preceded us have hidden their
principal intention under divers enigmas and innumerable equivoca-
tions to the end that the world may not be ruined by the publication
of their doctrine.'

The need for esotericism was not only enjoined verbally in alchemy
but was also symbolized by such well-known illustrations as the
Alchemical Citadel of Heinrich Khunrath. The Citadel stands in a circle which has twenty-one entrances, twenty of which have no way out,
being blocked by a great wall. There are twenty sections enumerating
the by-ways in which seekers can go astray. There is only one true path,
but even that is made hazardous by the difficulties to be overcome and,
in the final stages, for the so-far successful aspirant, the Philosophers'

Stone, the final prize, is in the centre guarded by a dragon which has to be overcome before winning through.

In Chinese alchemy the exoteric side, the *wei tan*, dealt with tangible ingredients, such as mercury, lead, realgar and cinnabar; it was a laboratory alchemy concerned with the transmutation of metals and the preparation of medicines and the drug, or elixir, of immortality. It was involved in scientific experiments and ultimately gave rise to the modern science of chemistry, making many interesting discoveries on the way. Esoteric alchemy, the *nei tan*, on the other hand, was only interested in the 'soul' of these substances and with the workings and operations of the body and soul of the aspirant, using yogic disciplines and methods and psychological practices. The *wei tan* was concerned with the material, the *nei tan* with the spiritual; the latter thus associated with religion rather than science. A Taoist alchemist of the first century AD said that the true lead is not the vulgar lead, but may be found in every house. 'If the secret is disclosed it will be so simple that everyone may get a good laugh.' In other words the lead is the psychological quality present in everyone.

Even though regarded as exoteric, the *wei tan* kept its recipes and instructions secret in that they were couched in symbolic terms and were withheld from the ignorant. Examples of esoteric names are 'Young-woman-along-the-river is not a female; Peach-male-lightness is not a male' (both are terms for mercury). Lead is 'Metal Lord,' or 'River Chariot.' Su Tung Po, who wrote a treatise on the Dragon and Tiger in AD 1110, said 'The Dragon is mercury; it is semen and blood. The Tiger is lead, it is the breath and bodily strength. Lead is also sperm and the blood mercury.' Among plants used Dragon's gall is gentian; Tiger's paws, jack-in-the-pulpit; Chicken heads, euryale; Rat tail, sage; Sky Dog, ginseng, and so on. As Ko Hung said, 'if we can be so confounded by common plants, how can we expect to comprehend arcane, recondite prescriptions?' This complaint was echoed centuries later in Europe by the French metallurgist Buffon, who said that in spite of reading and studying all the books on alchemy they had offered him 'nothing but obscurities and unintelligible processes.'

The disadvantage of esoteric knowledge and of keeping it secret is that it can be lost with the passing of the adept or custodian of that lore and the greater the knowledge or powers of the adept, the less likely it is that these will be handed down intact, it being unlikely that there would be a disciple of his own stature to fall heir to it.

When the esoteric is ignored or misunderstood, exotericism takes over completely and proliferates in outward forms; rituals and rites become meaningless and are performed mechanically for their own sake, providing spurious and superstitious conditions, which, having lost their value, merely make the performer feel safe in the protection of the congregation or crowd. The symbol then becomes a sign, having lost its inner significance. So, too, do science and technology now concentrate on the outward: machines, space travel, endless gadgets, instead of the inner study of mankind which, if developed, would reveal inner powers capable of achieving the same effects without the disadvantages of outward fragmentation and the consequent breakdown of human relationships. Humanity displays a genius for technical knowledge and mechanical invention, the exoteric, combined with an almost complete failure of adjustment and development in the character and understanding of the inner, the esoteric, world. The result is total frustration; conflict and war in national life, and in the personal sphere nervous illness, tension, imbalance and disharmony. The yin, esoteric, and the *yang,* exoteric, here as everywhere, require each other and must work together with Nature, not against her; co-operating, not 'conquering.'

16

THE TWO GREAT POWERS

The primary theme in creation mythology is the emergence from the One of the Two, the creation of the primordial pair and the beginning of duality. This male-female symbolism is basic to alchemy, since the male sulphur and the female quicksilver must work on and with each other in balanced relationship. They are different but complementary, seeking out each other to bring about the restoration of original wholeness. They must continually stimulate each other. In alchemy everything is growing and divided into sexes; the whole universe is a living being working towards perfection. The eternal reactions of humanity and Nature upon each other, the alternating *yin* and *yang* in growth and decline, the fusion of the objective and subjective, all give rise to the cyclic powers of change and produce the rhythms of the cosmos.

Duality is the very essence of life in the manifest world; the light and dark following earth's turning away from the sun and returning to the new dawn. Its opposite is present in every thing: little is harder or more solid than the flint that gives birth to the spark of fire, the most unstable and volatile of elements. In man and woman the two powers manifest themselves in duality not only in sex, but in each sex. Woman, the *yin,* is negative externally and positive internally; man, the *yang,* is positive externally and negative internally: each incorporate both powers. De Groot says: 'The hard and soft match and contain one another, *yang* gives and *yin* receives. The male and female need one another. It is this need that brings about creation-procreation, so that the essential *ch'i* may have its proper play.' He calls the two powers 'the Great Regulators of the cosmos which cause the phenomena of creation, evolution and destruction.' They are also called the Contraries, the Contending Dragons, the Great Extremes. The breath, vital essence, or *ch'i* of the *yin* and *yang* is necessary for creation of any form. The *Ts'an T'ung Ch'i* says that 'creation is dependent on the fusion of the breath of *yin* and *yang* . . . if a thing does not contain *yin* and *yang* it repudiates its origin. Baby chicks do not come from infertile eggs.'

In alchemy *yin* is coagulation and *yang* is solution; in metals *yin* is quicksilver and silver and *yang* is Sulphur and gold; *yin* the moon and earth, *yang* the sun and heavens, while in the work *yin* represents the esoteric and *yang* the exoteric. The processes of heating and cooling are also related to *yang* the sun and *yin*, the moon; they bring about change by balancing each other with their hardness and softness. In the *Ts'an T'ung Ch'i* the sun and moon are said to reach out for one another; they are 'the two great luminaries which arose from the Great Ultimate, the *T'ai Chi*. The *yang* evolved as air and formed the heavens, the *yin* coagulated to form the earth; particles from the *yang* formed the sun and *yin* particles the moon; between them they begat the stars. Thus the *yang* and *yin* are also known as *T'ien* and *Ti*, Heaven and Earth.'

All metals were regarded as the result of the union of the two powers, male and female, sulphur and quicksilver, spirit and soul; their union produced perfection: cinnabar. There is, however, a dual nature in quicksilver or mercury, which is consonant with the two natures of the feminine power, at once the nourisher of the embryo within the womb, the hermetic vessel, the vase, etc., and the death-dealing dissolvent, so that it brings life or death according to its particular situation. This lunar material is also the 'water of life,' which nourishes in the womb, and the destructive humid dissolution of death; but that which decomposes is also the medium for generation. As Synesius said: 'It is indeed that which decomposes and that which makes to generate.'

Metals were divided into the two sexes in smelting processes and young men and maidens took part in the rituals in which the 'marriage of the metals' was involved. In a memorial ode, on Ch'u Yuan, by Chia I, c. 170 BC, we read: 'Heaven and Earth are like a smelting furnace, the forces of natural change are the workmen, the *yin* and the *yang* are the fuel, and the Ten Thousand Things are the metal.' Fire for the furnace was also produced by the male-female interaction in the two 'rubbing sticks' which brought forth the vital spark; the fire was latent in the *yin* wood but was ignited by *yang* action.

In Shamanism, when working magic and transformations the shaman has his 'celestial wife' who acts as an instructor and protects and helps him. He is also assisted by a woman in the 'ascent to heaven,' or some symbolically feminine object can take her place. It is the female influence which not only helps him on his journey but enables him to emerge victorious. Also, apart from the *wu* and *hsi* female and male magicians, Chinese legend is full of magical and alchemical arts being taught by a female spirit or goddess. Here, again, we are reminded of the Yellow Emperor and his Three Immortal Maids and the daughters of the Emperor Yao, who taught the Emperor Shou (2258-2208) the magical art of 'flying like a bird.' In the West the alchemist had his female assistant, his *soror mystica,* to help him in his work. Pictures of the two working together appear frequently in alchemical texts and the ores on which they worked were produced by the union of the two powers of sulphur and mercury. The Emerald Tablet states: 'Sulphur, solar power, Mercury, lunar power, are the "father and mother" of the alchemical embryo.'

In western alchemy, in the imperfect state, the two powers work against each other, just as the contraries in life can be in conflict and produce dire results until they work together in unity. As Burckhardt says: 'Here we have the analogy of the love contest between man and woman; it is the feminine fascination which dissolves the "solidification" of the virile nature and wakens its power. It is sufficient to remark that it is this fascination, spiritually canalized, which plays a certain part in Tantric methods.' This 'love contest' appears also in western astrology in Venus and Mars, the Pair of Lovers, who complement each other in their signs, the old symbol for Mars being the circle surmounted by the cross ♂, with Venus as the circle above the cross ♀, both being a perfect union of the male-female powers. Burckhardt points out that the alchemical meaning of the planetary signs is identical with the astrological: 'Each planet possesses two adjacent "houses," a left and right, or feminine and masculine, with the exception of the moon and sun which have only one house each and rule respectively the feminine and masculine halves of the Zodiac.' The concept of the two great powers appears in many civilizations. In Egypt Isis and Osiris are the lunar and solar powers that brought forth all things, and the doctrine of the contrary powers, the positive sulphur and negative quicksilver, working on each other, is present in all alchemy. Zosimus writes of their interdependence: 'Above celestial things, below terrestrial things, by the male and the female the work is accomplished,' and in *Le Texte d'Alchymie* we read: 'Sulphur cannot be without Mercury, and Mercury cannot be without this Sulphur which is intimately united and incorporated with it, as the soul is with the body.' Nicholas Flamel says: 'In the second operation thou hast two conjoined and married natures, the masculine and the feminine; and they are fashioned in one sole body, which is the androgyne of the ancients.' This is the *conjunctio*, the union of sulphur and quicksilver, sun and moon, king and queen; the two together combining the blind strength of the male with the subtle intuition of the female, of action and thought, method and wisdom, of all the opposites which together bring mankind back to the primordial unity and perfection.

In the interplay between the two, sulphur effects the coagulation of the body in dryness and hardness, masculine qualities, and therefore requires modification and purification in the dissolving and softening qualities of quicksilver, the feminine power, which helps sulphur to rid itself of its undesirable features and to reveal its noble aspect; this is the Tantric play of the feminine on the masculine which wakens its active power. Sulphur also symbolizes the rigid, rational and theoretical outlook of knowledge which is sterile until dissolved by the intuitional, instinctive feminine understanding symbolized by quicksilver. In Hinduism, *Purusha*, the male, the contemplative intelligence, is 'the great impotent one' who needs *Prakriti*, the female, generative, intuitional, to activate it. A similar interaction is found in Buddhism.

Though the western religious-philosophical thought, based largely on Aristotelian dualism, asserted that the two powers were initially in conflict, the *yin-yang* symbolism of the East had no such dichotomy; the two powers are held in harmonious tension, and though called opposites they are, as Pu Cheng said, 'incapable of mutual negation.' The dualism of Heaven and Earth was resolved into the unity of the Parent, spoken of as the Father-and-Mother of all creatures. In a Great Declaration, at the beginning of the Chou Dynasty (1122 BC), it was stated: 'The Heavens are representatives of divine majesty, the Earth is representative of divine care: the former teaches paternal authority, the latter the more-than-maternal love.' Confucius, in the *Li Chi*, said: 'Man is the product of the attributes of Heaven and Earth by the interactions of the dual forces of Nature, the union of the animal and intelligent souls.' Humanity is frequently spoken of as 'a miniature Heaven and Earth,' a product of the powers of *yin* and *yang*, a microcosm which is a reflection of the macrocosm. Like Heaven and Earth, the two great powers cannot be separated; one implies the other, they cannot be thought of in total separation. The two opposites, contrary but complementary, bind and neutralize each other without a diminution of either; together they produce perfection, which is gold in alchemical terms and in classical Taoism 'the Return to the Source,' union with the Tao.

The fact that each sex is only half accounts for the universally expressed need, often amounting to an acute longing, to find the complementary partner, the 'other half,' a completion, the regaining on the personal level of union and wholeness. From the alchemical aspect, the union is spiritual rather than sexual, it is metaphysical in significance, transcending the personal and emotional state and unifying on a higher level. Each individual has also the two powers within; in the unregenerate state of the base metal they are in conflict and are in the position of a kingdom divided against itself. In this disharmony the *yin* and *yang* are out of balance, not only in the individual but in the world in general, which is, naturally, only as good as the individuals of which it is composed. The old, base nature must die and much of alchemical symbolism deals with death; everything must die before it can be renewed, a theme found in all initiatory traditions. In alchemy, the minerals die in the stove or athanor, to be fused and ultimately united; this is also the 'marriage' of the metals and marriage is also associated with death in dying to the old life in which each partner 'gives up' to the other. In the fusion of sulphur and quicksilver each loses its individual identity to take on the united character of both. But death is always a reunion, body to earth, soul to the realm of spirit; it is a transmutation and transformation.

Continuing the marriage symbolism, Burckhardt writes: 'Man and woman, who in natural fashion incarnate the two poles of the alchemical work, sulphur and quicksilver, can by their mutual love—when this is spiritually heightened and internalized—develop the cosmic power, or power of the soul which operates the alchemical dissolution and coagulation;' or, again as Artephius wrote: 'They will embrace in such a way that never again will they be separable one from another. Then indeed will the spirit unite with the body in perfect harmony, so that together they become an immortal thing.' The male-female symbolism employed is merely a support for the esoteric understanding of what is involved in the work: the supreme aim being that of unity and return to primordial perfection.

17

THE REAL ALCHEMY

That the real alchemy was concerned with the metaphysical, mystical and religious life is made abundantly clear in the writings of leading alchemists of both East and West who state categorically: 'Our gold is not of this world.' All the exhortations to right conduct, purity and religious observances show that the Work was, for the true alchemist, a spiritual matter.

Writing on yoga and alchemy and discussing the legends and references in Tantrism, Eliade says: 'We have here no pre-chemistry, no science in embryo, but a spiritual technique, which, while operating on "matter", sought first of all to "perfect the spirit", to bring about deliverance and autonomy . . . gold is the one perfect solar metal and hence its symbolism meets the symbolism of Spirit, of spiritual freedom.' This is confirmed by John Blofeld who, travelling in pre-Communist China and visiting Buddhist and Taoist monasteries, received from a Taoist abbot the statement:

Ours is not a religion but a way to the Way . . . our yogas and meditation begin with the generating of tranquillity, that in the stillness of our hearts we may apprehend the Tao within, around, above and below us. We seek to nourish our vitality and prolong our lives in order to gain more time for the refinement of spirit needed for attaining the higher goals. Then comes the compounding of the Golden Pill which some misguided persons have sought to produce by alchemical processes, whereas in truth it can be compounded only within the body and is therefore known esoterically as the immortal foetus. We Taoists are generally agreed that its creation is the means to immortality, but at this point paths diverge, some seek aeon-long immortality, the attainment of a god-like state, as an end in itself; others strive to Return to the Source, an apotheosis identical with the attainment of Nirvana, though conceptions of the inconceivable naturally differ.

In the spiritual alchemy even the pursuit of longevity had its origins in the idea that the longer the physical life, the longer the time for attaining spiritual transformation into the True Man and becoming one with the Tao; to this end the alchemist had to transmute the base metal of the physical desires into the pure gold of the spiritual. From the *Shen Hsien Chuan* comes the instruction: 'If you are bent on attaining immortality, begin by getting rid of the body-spirits. As soon as they are gone you will gain fixity of will-power and freedom from passion and desire.'

Waley, in his 'Notes on Chinese Alchemy' dismisses the theory that alchemy was a pre-chemistry and pithily expresses it as: 'Alchemy, on the rare occasions when it has been made the subject of reasonable enquiry, has usually been studied as part of what one may call the pre-history of science. But if, to use a favourite phrase, we are to see in alchemy merely "the cradle of chemistry," are we not likely, whatever its initial charm, to lose patience with an infancy protracted through some fifteen centuries?' The true alchemy was, in fact, an applied science or art (spoken of as either by its adherents) in the control of the elements affecting life and Nature and humanity in a spiritual development; it was called, as Taylor puts it, 'a chemistry of the spirit.' 'Let alchemy be called a "chemistry of the spirit" and it will be possible to understand its many aspects and the conflicting views of those who have not grasped its essential features.' If it were only gold-or-pill making and early science, it is remarkable that as Professor Sivin points out, 'there were many treatises which give no directions for making anything,' and if it were merely the search for gold, why the universal reference to 'our gold' as being something distinct from the common gold?

The search for gold was the search for wisdom, for the knowledge of the necessary transformation of unregenerate humanity into the Sage or integrated being, expressed as 'the opaque becomes luminous.' Roger Bacon said that 'Nature has always had for an end and tries incessantly to reach perfection, that is gold.' In Vedic tradition 'gold is immortality;' that is, the incorruptible spirit, the illuminated being. The colouring, or tincture, represents the colouring of the unregenerate or base nature with the divine. In Europe Fludd said: 'Be ye transmuted from mortal to living philosophers' stones . . . Indeed, every pious and righteous man is a spiritual alchemist . . . who . . . understands not only how to distinguish but with the fire of the divine Spirit to separate the false from the true . . . for only this way is unclean lead turned to gold.' The medieval 'Rosarium' says: 'Our gold is not the common gold' and 'the philosopher is not the master of the stone but rather its minister.' Then yet again, 'Our gold is not in any way the gold of the multitude, but is the living gold . . . it is wisdom.'

The real alchemy was the search for wisdom; its work was esoteric and on the individual, not in the laboratory, or rather the body is the laboratory in which the knowledge of the Self is gained. That the quest was spiritual, not material, is attested by alchemy's religious affiliations, to Taoism, in particular, in the East; there are also constant references to it in Hinduism and Buddhism and strong associations in the Babylonian and Chaldean civilizations, the Egyptian-Greek hermeticism and, later, in Christianity and Islam. Alchemy is also essentially mystical since its aim is union, the end of duality and absorption in the Absolute. Alchemical terms are used throughout for spiritual processes; the *conjunctio* is the same as the mystic's union with the One, the loss of individual identity with the limitations of the ego dissolved in the perfect whole, and again the base metal, transmuted by purification and refining, becomes the gold of perfection, of wisdom. The alchemist Alipili wrote:

> The highest wisdom consists in this, for man to know himself . . . therefore let the high enquirers and searchers into the deep mysteries of nature first learn to know what they have in themselves, and by the divine power within them let them first heal themselves and transmute their souls . . . if that which thou seekest thou findest not within thee thou will never find it without thee . . . He who desires the primacy among students of nature will nowhere find a greater or better field of study than himself. Therefore will I from certain true experience proclaim: 'Oh man, know thyself, in thee is hid the treasure of treasures.'

The study of man and Nature cannot be separated. As the alchemist worked on Nature so he could not avoid working on himself. As Hopkins says: 'To Aristotle organic nature was like man. But to the alchemist *all* nature was like man; the spiritual overshadowing the material, and reproduction, the greatest of all mysteries, was possible only when the body of the metal was endowed with excess of the spiritual.' Sendivogius uses the symbolism of the mirror: 'The Sage sees Heaven reflected in Nature as in a mirror; and he pursues this Art not for the sake of gold or silver, but for the love of knowledge which it reveals.' The microcosm and macrocosm reflect each other but are one, there is no difference between humanity and the cosmos. 'The natural world is only an image and material copy of a heavenly and spiritual pattern; that is, the very existence of this world is based upon the reality of its celestial archetype.' Again, this is the hermetic 'As above, so below,' or, 'In truth, certainly and without doubt, whatever is below is like that which is above, and whatever is above is like that which is below.' This enunciates the law of correspondences: that all creation is, in fact, a reflection; the phenomenal reflects the spiritual. The hermetic tradition also says that 'The work . . . is to be found within you and is enduring: you will always have it present, wherever you are, on land or on sea.'

Meditation was an important factor in Chinese alchemy in developing the 'inner elixir,' and the sealed vase was the isolated mountain retreat, hermitage, or meditation room, where knowledge of the inner self was attained, where transformation took place and from which the new man was born; hence the constant reference to the foetus or the seed as also symbolically the birth of this new being. There is pre-natal growth in the seclusion of the closed room or retreat, the womb, before the new being emerges from darkness to light, from dependence to independence, into the life of the spirit. A modern Taoist Master called this foetus 'an incorporeal manifestation of the union of spirit with vitality,' and a Japanese professor, visiting the Taoist White Cloud monastery in the 1940s, found the ancient values still alive:

Little significance was attached to the artificial, so-called cultural, activities. Taking pride in gathering scraps of knowledge, conducting surveys, doing research—those may be efforts to find some satisfaction or self-understanding in the society of men, but they end, as does life, like the flaring out of a candle. It is better to be embraced in the vastness of Nature, to melt into it. Then there is no wasted resistance to life, no useless conflagration. When one's breathing is in harmony with nature, one becomes identical with its very life-flow.

Alchemists of both East and West state categorically that Nature is their guide and exemplar, that they are working with her and following her laws. In alchemy they may be hastening some of her processes, but never working against her. As a science alchemy aimed at the understanding of the properties and formations of mineral substances; as a spiritual art or philosophy it was concerned with the mysteries of life and the cosmos. It had a cosmological relationship with every aspect of life, human, animal, plant and mineral. One could not go wrong in following Nature. As the Golden Tract says: 'Nature seeks and demands the gradual attainment of perfection, and a general approximation to the highest standard of purity and excellence.'

The cult of longevity was not considered to be going against living in accord with Nature since she had long-lived creatures whose life span greatly outdid that of the human being; in any case, it would be Nature herself who provided the life-giving plants and substances; the individual had only to find and use them. Moreover, the aim of a long life for the true alchemist was a spiritual one, the gaining of time in the body for the development of the spirit.

Eliade writes that 'Alchemy represents the projection of a drama, at once cosmic and spiritual, in laboratory terms. The aim of the *opus magnum* was at once the freeing of the human soul and the healing of the cosmos.' In ancient India the Master Nagarguna made it clear that the work was a spiritual technique when he said: 'The mercurial system must not be looked upon as a simple eulogy of metal, for it is our means . . . of attaining the supreme goal, which is deliverance;' and in an ancient Chinese text he is also reported as answering the question: 'It is believed that it is possible to make gold from stones; is that not absurd?' by saying 'It is perfectly possible in the spiritual sense.'

The whole work of alchemy is summed up in the phrase 'To make of the body a spirit and of the spirit a body;' or, variously expressed, it is 'the spiritualization of the body and the embodiment of the spirit;' or, again, it is 'to spiritualize matter and materialize spirit.' In the hermetic tradition this is enunciated as 'We receive not only a new soul with this regeneration but also a new body . . . it is more spiritual than the air, akin to the rays of the Sun which penetrates all bodies, and as different from the old body as the resplendent Sun is from the dark earth.'

The goal of the Taoist alchemist-mystic was transformation, or perhaps more correctly, transfiguration of the whole body until it ceases to 'be' and is absorbed into and becomes the Tao. The alchemist becomes the True Man, returning to the Source—the Taoist phrase for universal Oneness.

NOTES

Chapter One:

1. *Autobiography,* tr. J. R. Ware.

Chapter Two:

1. Concerning the Nature of Things.
2. From a Rosicrucian Manual, *Kompass der Weisen* (1782).

Chapter Six:

1. From the *Ts'an T'ung Ch'i* of Wei Po-yang, tr. Wu and Davis, *Isis.* Vol. XVIII (1932).
2. *Speculum Alkionia Minus.*
3. *Opus Major.*

Chapter Seven:

1. Ko Hung, *Pao P'u Tzu.* XVI.
2. Needham, *Science and Civilization in China,* Vol. V.
3. Ko Hung, *Pao P'u Tzu.*

Chapter Nine:

1. From the *Ts'an T'ung Ch'i.*

BIBLIOGRAPHY

Blofeld, John. *The Secret and the Sublime* (Allen and Unwin, 1973).

Burckhardt, Titus. *Alchemy* (Stuart and Watkins, 1967).

———, 'Insight into Alchemy,' *Studies in Comparative Religion* (Autumn 1979).

Chevalier, Jean (ed.). *Dictionnaire des Symbols* (Paris, 1973).

Chkashige, Masumi. *Oriental Alchemy* (Weiser, New York, 1974 [1936]).

Chung-yuan Chang. *Creativity as Process in Taoism* (Eranos Jahrbuch, Zurich, 1956).

Da Liu. *The Tao and Chinese Culture* (RKP, 1981).

Dubs, H. H. 'The Beginnings of Alchemy,' *Isis,* Vol. 38 (1947-8).

Eliade, Mircea. *Yoga, Immortality and Freedom* (Pantheon Books, 1958).

———, *The Forge and the Crucible* (Rider, 1962).

Fung yu-lan. *The Spirit of Chinese Philosophy* (RKP, 1947).

Gettings, F. *Dictionary of Occult, Hermetic and Experimental Sigils* (RKP, 1981).

Giles, Lionel. *A Gallery of Chinese Immortals* (John Murray, 1948).

de Groot, J. J. M. *The Religious Systems of China* (Leyden, 1892-1907).

Harrison, R. *The Measure of Life* (Stanley Nott, 1936).

Holmyard, E. J. *Alchemy* (Pelican, 1957, 1968).

Hopkins, A. J. *Alchemy, Child of Greek Philosophy* (New York, 1967).

Johnson, O. S. *Gold. A Study of Chinese Alchemy* (New York, 1974).

Jung, C. J. *Psychology and Alchemy* (RKP, 1953).

Legeza, Lazzlo. *Tao Magic* (Pantheon, 1975).

Lu-ch'iang Wu & Davis, T. L. 'The Ts'an T'ung Ch'i of Wei Po-yang,' *Isis,* Vol. 18 (1932).

Needham, Joseph. *Science and Civilization in China* (CUP; 1954).

Read, John. 'Alchemy and Alchemists,' *Folklore,* Vol. XLIII (1933).

Redgrave, H. S. *Alchemy: Ancient and Modern* (E. P. Publishing Co., 1917, 1973).

Shigeru Nakayama. 'Characteristics of Chinese Astrology,' *Isis*, Vol. 57 (1966).

Silberer, Herbert. *Hidden Symbolism of Alchemy and the Occult Arts* (Dover, 1971).

Sivin, Nathan. *Chinese Alchemy: Preliminary Studies* (Harvard UP, 1968).

Spooner, R. C. & Wang, C. H. 'The Divine Nine Turn Tan Sha Method: A Chinese Alchemical Recipe,' *Isis*, Vol. 38 (1947-8).

Taylor, F. S. *The Alchemists* (Heinemann, 1951).

Thorndike, Lynn. *History of Magic and Experimental Science*, Vol. 1 (Macmillan, 1923).

Valois, Nicholas (compiled by Bernard Roger). *Les Cinq Livres, ou la clef du secret des secrets* (Paris, 1975).

Ware, J. R. (tr.) *Alchemy, Medicine, Religion in the China of AD 320* (The *Nei P'ien* of Ko Hung [Pao Pu Tzu]) (MIT Press, 1966).

Warner, E. T. C. *Myths and Legends of China* (Harrap, 1922).

Welch, H. and Seidel, A. (ed.) *Facets of Taoism* (Yale University Press, 1979).

Wing-tsit Chan. *A Source Book of Chinese Philosophy* (Princeton University Press, 1963).

INDEX

TO OUR READERS

Weiser Books, an imprint of Red Wheel/Weiser, publishes books across the entire spectrum of occult, esoteric, speculative, and New Age subjects. Our mission is to publish quality books that will make a difference in people's lives without advocating any one particular path or field of study. We value the integrity, originality, and depth of knowledge of our authors.

Our readers are our most important resource, and we appreciate your input, suggestions, and ideas about what you would like to see published.

Visit our website at *www.redwheelweiser.com* to learn about our upcoming books and free downloads, and be sure to go to *www.redwheelweiser.com/newsletter/* to sign up for newsletters and exclusive offers.

You can also contact us at *info@rwwbooks.com* or at

Red Wheel/Weiser, LLC
65 Parker Street, Suite 7
Newburyport, MA 01950